HUDSON'S BAY
COMPANY ADVENTURES

HUDSON'S BAY COMPANY ADVENTURES

Tales of Canada's Fur Traders

ELLE ANDRA-WARNER

VICTORIA · VANCOUVER · CALGARY

Heritage House Publishing Company Ltd.
#108 – 17665 66A Avenue
Surrey, BC V3S 2A7
www.heritagehouse.ca

Heritage House Publishing Company Ltd.
PO Box 468
Custer, WA
98240-0468

Library and Archives Canada Cataloguing in Publication
Andra-Warner, Elle, 1946 –
    Hudson's Bay Company adventures: the rollicking saga of Canada's fur traders / Elle Andra-Warner.—1st Heritage House ed.

ISBN 978-1-894974-68-4

    1. Hudson's Bay Company—History. 2. Fur trade—Canada—History. 3. Frontier and pioneer life—Canada. I. Title.

FC3207.A53 2009   971.2'01   C2008-908133-1

Originally published 2003 by Altitude Publishing Canada Ltd.

Library of Congress Control Number: 2009920315

Series editor: Lesley Reynolds.
Cover design: Chyla Cardinal. Interior design: Frances Hunter.
Cover photo: Glenbow Archives (NA-1041-6). Interior photos: Hudson Bay Archives/Provincial Archives of Manitoba, page 27 (HBCA P-380) and page 93 (1987/363-C-11A/779); Glenbow Archives, page 108 (NA-77-1).

 Mixed Sources
Cert no. SW-COC-001271
© 1996 FSC
FSC

The interior of this book was printed on 100% post-consumer recycled paper, processed chlorine free and printed with vegetable-based inks.

Heritage House acknowledges the financial support for its publishing program from the Government of Canada through the Book Publishing Industry Development Program (BPIDP), Canada Council for the Arts and the province of British Columbia through the British Columbia Arts Council and the Book Publishing Tax Credit.

BRITISH COLUMBIA ARTS COUNCIL

The Canada Council | Le Conseil des Arts
for the Arts | du Canada

12 11 10 09   1 2 3 4 5

Printed in Canada

To Canada's pioneers and First Nations,
whose stories continue to inspire us
with their spirit of adventure

Contents

Prologue

IT WAS A TRAGIC DAY *at Seven Oaks, Manitoba. On June 19, 1816, the Métis leader, Cuthbert Grant, and his men were armed for war and many wore war paint. As their captain general, Grant was leading over 60 Métis on horseback to capture the Hudson's Bay Company's Fort Douglas, the centre of Selkirk's Red River settlement.*

There was no surprise element to the attack. The colony's Governor Semple, a Boston-born Loyalist, had been warned about an attack, but had chosen to ignore the warning. Semple believed diplomacy was all that was needed to defuse the situation. His plan was to meet the attackers and read them the proclamation forbidding Métis to commit acts of violence against the colony.

When Grant and his mounted riders arrived, the Métis leader halted his men at the group of trees known as Seven Oaks. They positioned themselves in a half-moon formation. At the same time, Semple led about 30 volunteers, on foot, out of the fort. In single file, they walked across the field to meet the Métis.

The Métis began to tighten their half-circle, manoeuvring Semple and his men towards the riverbank. Grant signalled a Métis named François Boucher to order Governor Semple and his men to lay down their arms—or be shot. Boucher slowly brought his horse forward. Semple strode forward to meet him and boldly seized the bridle of Boucher's horse. Grant trained his gun on Semple.

A heated discussion developed. "What do you want?" asked Boucher in broken English. "What do you want?" said Semple, throwing the question back to Boucher. "We want our fort," was the reply. "Well, go to your fort!" Semple yelled back.

There was a scuffle as Semple tried to seize Boucher's gun. A shot rang out. Grant, who still had his gun on the governor—pulled the trigger—wounding Semple in the thigh.

And the fierce competition for the fur trade became warfare.

1

From the Beaver
to the HBC

THE STORY OF THE NORTH AMERICAN fur trade started over 500 years ago. It started because of a demand for hats—men's fashionable felt hats—hats made of beaver pelts.

Back in the sixteenth century, the beavers of Europe and most of Russia had been trapped almost to extinction to satisfy the demand for beaver hats in England. When European hatters, by chance, discovered the superb fur of the beavers in North America, they clamoured to get the fur to make their felt. The richest, most luxuriant beaver pelts came from the cold, far north regions of North America. And the hatters wanted them.

The Native peoples welcomed fur trade with Europeans. They willingly traded their beaver coats and pelts for goods that made their lives easier, such as kettles, knives and guns.

This lucrative market for northern beaver fuelled the fierce rivalry between the English and the French and led to the formation of one of the world's oldest commercial empires—the Hudson's Bay Company (HBC).

The Hat That Started It All

The wearing of hats in Europe began in the 1300s, but it would be another 100 years before they became popular. Men were the first to adopt hats as an important fashion item. Men's beaver hats were first made using the actual beaver skins. The "felted" hats appeared in continental Europe around 1456 and about 50 years later in England. The craze skyrocketed in the 1600s with the introduction of the fine fur of the Canadian beaver. Men's hats were more than a statement of fashion. They were indicators of the wearer's social position. The hat symbolized the wearer's authority, hierarchy and importance. The bigger the hat, the higher one's status.

The best hats were made from the fur of beaver pelts. They produced a dense, durable, waterproof felt with a lustrous silky sheen. And the European hatters discovered that the very best beaver pelts came from the "coat beaver" worn by Native peoples in North America. The Native peoples made their coats by sewing six to eight pelts together as a robe, using sinew for thread. They wore the fur side of the pelts next to their body. The sweat of their bodies, mixed with the smoke of their lodges, made the inside fur soft and supple with a silky sheen. The pelt's long "guard hairs" would fall out leaving only the soft "underfur." This prized downy fur was used to make the beaver hats.

The first of the popular men's cocked hats were the cavalier hats of the 1600s. Painters presented romantic images of cavaliers in England and musketeers in France wearing these hats. The wide-brimmed beaver hats were trimmed with ostrich plumes and jewellery, and one side of the brim was usually cocked or rolled. Although they were very impressive, the droopy brims were a hazard for horse riding and sword fighting.

As men's hats became more of a status symbol, the cocked beaver hats grew bigger and higher. The classic tricorne hats of the 1700s became popular in the American and French Revolutions, and were worn by gentlemen and courtiers throughout Europe, as well as by pirates. Around 1790, the bicorne hat also became the fashion choice for artists and intellectuals. In addition, it was the military dress hat of the British, the Americans and the French. The bicorne hat was the signature hat of Napoleon Bonaparte.

For over 200 years, making hats with beaver felt was a flourishing industry. Good hatters made roughly nine hats a week. Five different groups of workers carried out 36 separate steps to produce one beaver hat. Tasks were arranged by gender. Women were responsible for preparing the fibres and doing the finishing work. Men were responsible for bowing the fur into batts, felting and fulling the batts into hats, and blocking, shaving, dyeing, stiffening and waterproofing them. The finest quality beaver hats had 9 to 12 ounces of pure fur in them. It took four beaver pelts to produce one pound of the fine, soft underfur.

The world of hat making was full of secret formulas and rivalries. Hat shops developed exclusive processes and mixtures. If an employee revealed these trade secrets to a competitor's shop, the punishment could be death.

And there was always the danger of the mad hatter syndrome—heavy metal poisoning from mercury. The pelts were soaked in a solution of mercury (mercuric oxide) to make the fur come off the pelts easily (called carroting because it gave fibres an orange tint). The mercury in the steam coming off the felt attacked the central nervous system of those involved in the felting and fulling of the hats. Hence the term "mad as a hatter."

Before the fur trade started, there were roughly six million beavers in Canada. During the peak of the fur trade, more than 200,000 pelts a year were sold to the European markets. Most were used to make fashionable beaver hats. The value of a beaver hat depended on the supply of pelts and the demand for them. At the peak of the beaver hat's popularity, a hat would cost the equivalent of six months' wages for a skilled worker. Fathers passed their beaver hats down to their sons. The beaver hat was so valuable that in 1659 Nantucket Island was purchased for £30 and two beaver hats, one for Governor Thomas Mayhew and one for his wife.

The cocked hat fell out of fashion in the 1800s and was replaced by the tall, polished stovepipe hat with its small rolled brim. The beaver-pelt supply was eventually depleted in North America—silk plush replaced beaver fur—and the frenzied era of beaver hats drew to a close.

Although beaver hats were, for many years, the fashion rage in Europe, few Europeans had ever seen a live beaver or knew anything about the animal or its amazing engineering feats.

The Incredible Canadian Beaver

The demand for beaver fur was the catalyst for the expansion of the fur trade in North America. And it was the beaver that set the course for Canadian history.

The stocky, roly-poly beaver is the second largest rodent in the world (the capybara of South America is first). The rotund adult weighs from 16 to 32 kilograms and measures 1.3 metres long. Its legs are short so it moves slowly on land. But in the water, the beaver is a swift and graceful swimmer. Using its 30-centimetre tail as a four-way rudder it can bullet up to 7 kilometres per hour. It has huge chisel-like teeth. These bright orange, enamelled teeth are constantly growing and—if the teeth are not worn down by gnawing—they will eventually pierce the beaver's skull and the beaver will perish.

Beavers are known for their incredible construction feats. They are superb architects, builders and planners that manage their own environment. They build themselves snug lodges with entrances and interiors that include a feeding chamber, dry nest den and a built-in ventilation system for fresh air. Their bedding consists of padded-down twigs and wide blades of grass, which they change regularly. A family of five or six beavers can live comfortably in the lodge.

After freezing weather begins, the beaver plasters the lodge with mud, except for the air intake near the top. This makes a concrete-like outer shell that only humans can break. To further protect the lodge, the beaver controls the water at specific levels by building a network of beaver dams. Built of sticks, rocks and mud in the river bed, the dams can be massive. They create deep ponds where the industrious beaver stores his winter food (chiefly birch, cottonwood, poplar, willow and young bark).

To complete its wilderness habitat, the beaver builds an incredibly complex canal system, a marvelous engineering feat. Ditches divert water and collect seepage from swamps. The canals can be 1.5 metres wide, 1 metre deep and more than 182 metres long. The system provides an easy transportation route for food supplies.

According to early journals, beavers became pets at some of the HBC posts. Samuel Hearne, while he was governor of Fort Prince of Wales (1775–82), included several beavers in his miniature private zoo. He wrote that his beavers became so domesticated that they answered to their names and followed him around. "They were as pleased at being fondled as any animal I ever saw. During the winter they lived on the same food as the women and were remarkably fond of rice and plum pudding." Fur trader Edward Umfreville also wrote about a beaver as a pet, "I once possessed a young male which, after a month's keeping, would follow me about like a dog; and when I had been absent from him for a couple of hours, he would show as much joy at my return as one of the canine species could possibly do."

The magnificent beaver attained official status as an emblem of Canada and was recognized as a symbol of the sovereignty of Canada by Royal Assent in a 1975 Act.

Indigenous Trappers and Traders

For eons, northern Native peoples had been trapping the beaver and efficiently using all the parts—the skins for clothing, the meat for food and the castoreum for medicine. Beaver pelts were bartered to other Native groups in well-established trade networks throughout the continent. Initially, the Europeans were simply another trading partner in an already successful system. Even before the Egyptian pyramids were built and before Cleopatra became queen of Egypt, business was already booming in North America between its Native peoples.

Each year, they would gather at destinations across North America to trade, fish, celebrate and, sometimes, mourn. Trading links, as well as natural river and lake waterway routes, were well established.

Kay-Nah-Chi-Wan-Nung was one of those ancient gathering places. It was located on North America's oldest highway, *Gete Miikana* (Ojibway for The Old Road). This travel route stretched from northern Minnesota to the Manitoba border. For over 6,000 years, *Gete Miikana* had been connecting a vibrant continent-wide trading network. Thousands paddled each year to Kay-Nah-Chi-Wan-Nung, setting up temporary villages along the shores of the Rainy River.

With spears and hooks, Native people fished for lake sturgeon that weighed up to 180 kilograms and reached 4 metres in length. They planted summer gardens for late harvesting. Men played the traditional moccasin game (a brilliant and complicated game that could go on for days). And they traded through a complex bartering system. Obsidian from Wyoming. Copper from Lake Superior. Marine shells from Florida. Turquoise from the southwestern United States. Flint from the Dakotas. Eulachon fish oil from the Pacific. Furs from the north.

Native economic networks connected trading systems, while tribes that became middlemen developed trading empires. For example, the Mandan trading empire once covered a huge area of North America, north from present-day Saskatchewan and Alberta, east to Lake of the Woods (near Kay-Nah-Chi-Wan-Nung), and from the

Missouri River to Mexico. These were no amateur traders. They were sophisticated, shrewd middlemen, hosting trade fairs and developing solid product lines, and they were canny traders. It was common for them to buy a horse from one trading partner and sell it to another partner for double its price.

Arrival of New Trade Partners

When the Europeans arrived in northern Canada, they encountered careful Native buyers. The Native peoples knew how to negotiate between English and French traders. They refused trade items they considered unnecessary, such as dolls and raisins. They did not hesitate to refuse unsatisfactory merchandise. Faulty guns and water-damaged tobacco were quickly detected. The Native traders demanded customer service from the Europeans and usually got it.

The Native peoples taught the Europeans about wilderness geography, transportation and survival. They taught them how to make snowshoes, birchbark canoes, moccasins and toboggans. And they showed them the best natural waterway routes. They also taught the early traders about the habits of the animals they needed for food and showed them how to make clothing from deer and caribou hides. In addition, the Native peoples showed the Europeans how to harvest rice and make pemmican, a pounded mixture of dried meat, fat and berries, which became the staple food of the inland fur trade.

From the beginning, the fur trade was based on an effective trading relationship between Europeans and the Native peoples. This successful relationship was the key to the traders' ability to satisfy Europe's demand for beaver. It is amazing to think that an article of clothing, the beaver hat, was the impetus for thousands of *coureurs du bois* (wood runners) and European trader-adventurers to press further and further into the wilderness. As they pushed the geographical boundaries in their quest, these merchant adventurers risked their reputations and their lives in a quest for the fur of the Canadian beaver.

CHAPTER

2

The Launch of a Trading Empire

THE ORIGIN OF THE GREAT trading empire of the Hudson's Bay Company can be traced back to two daring, renegade French fur traders. Pierre-Esprit Radisson and his brother-in-law, Médard Chouart, Sieur des Groseilliers, embarked on their historic voyage to the New World on two small ketches, the *Nonsuch* and the *Eaglet*.

Radisson and des Groseilliers had a dream—to harvest the untouched wealth in beaver and other furs from the vast northern interior of Canada. They envisioned a fur-trading system in which ocean-going ships would sail from Europe into the Hudson Bay to collect furs in abundance from permanent trading posts. These furs would fall into their hands through trade with the Cree and other northern Native groups. Radisson and des Groseilliers' ultimate goal? Huge profits.

A Plan Evolves

To put their plan in motion, they needed a successful first voyage to Hudson Bay to convince investors of the potential. But first they needed investors to fund it. Their dream of creating a fur-trading empire began in the early 1650s, in the backcountry of the area now known as the Great Lakes. Des Groseilliers, a shrewd, tough and influential fur trader in Trois-Rivières, had heard stories from Native people about a rich, untouched beaver country north of Lake Superior. The stories intrigued him. Over the years, he began piecing together information about the northern fur bonanza from his Native trading partners.

Competition for new trade routes was fierce among the French fur traders, who were all trying to find new routes to increase their supply of beaver pelts. But the colonial French government, which held power, made the rules and regulations for licensing traders. And des Groseilliers, particularly, didn't like being told what to do by anyone.

By August 1659, des Groseilliers and Radisson were determined to reach the Great Lakes with their Native trading partners. They needed this inland trip to position themselves for their Hudson Bay project. Their first request to the governor of New France to accompany Hurons into the interior was refused. However, their second request to accompany six Saulteaux was approved—on the condition that a Jesuit priest accompany them—an unacceptable restriction for the independent-minded des Groseilliers.

A Stealthy Departure

Rather than be burdened with a Jesuit priest, Radisson and des Groseilliers slipped away one summer night in 1659. They joined Saulteaux guides who were waiting for them along the St. Lawrence River. Their stealthy departure started a chain of events that would take them, 10 years later, to the Hudson Bay and eventually lead to the formation of the Hudson's Bay Company.

The unlicensed journey was treacherous. New France was at war with the Iroquois and attacks were frequent. But des Groseilliers was experienced in fighting and in winning against the Iroquois. His courage and confidence were respected by his Native partners. He was even considered a "warrior chief" because of his ability to successfully break through Iroquois ambushes by direct assault (one time concealing himself behind bales of fur).

By October 1659, they had reached the extreme southwest of Lake Superior. They wintered with the Saulteaux, Menominee and Dakotas and fought alongside their Saulteaux allies against the Iroquois. Radisson and des Groseilliers' relationship with the Native peoples was based on trust. They even participated in the traditional Algonquin "Feast of the Dead" held in Saulteaux territory at the end of the winter. Over 2,000 persons from 18 different nations attended the 14-day ceremonies.

During the feast, Radisson and des Groseilliers witnessed the Grand Assembly of the Algonquin peoples and watched as peace was concluded between the Sioux and Cree tribes. Radisson and des Groseilliers addressed the nations gathered at the feast to talk about the benefits of establishing lasting trade relations with them. The two Frenchmen established a small trading fort in the territory.

A year later, on August 19, 1660, Radisson and des Groseilliers returned to Trois-Rivières. Behind them was a flotilla of 60 canoes, over 300 Assiniboine and bales of the glossiest beaver pelts ever brought to New France. They were now ready to ask the governor of New France for ships and financial support for their next expedition, a voyage to the Hudson Bay. They returned from their inland journey convinced that the bay could be reached by way of the Atlantic Ocean.

On the return that August, Radisson wrote, "We finally reached Quebec . . . we were greeted by several cannon salvos from the fort's battery and from some ships anchored in the harbour. These ships would have returned to France empty if we had not shown up."

But the response they received from the governor shocked them. Not only did the governor confiscate most of their pelts, he levied huge taxes on their furs for having left the colony without first obtaining his permission.

Des Groseilliers was furious. He sailed to France and took his case to a higher court, eventually winning. The money he had paid in taxes was returned.

A Radical Change of Direction

In the summer of 1661, des Groseilliers sailed back to New France, and he and Radisson made a momentous decision. They decided to take their radical Hudson Bay fur-trading proposal to the English. First, they looked for support among the Boston merchants in New England. They secured some financing and made an aborted trip to the Hudson Bay with Zachary Gillam as captain. Their voyage, however, caught the attention of Sir George Cartaret, an influential member of the court of King Charles II of England. He invited the pair to present their plan to the king. In 1665, they set sail for England.

But misfortune followed them. While sailing across the Atlantic Ocean, their ship was captured by Dutch privateers and they were held as prisoners. Later they were put ashore in Spain and finally made their way to England.

The England they found in the autumn of 1665 was a desperate, depressing place. Sailing up the Thames River to London, they passed smoke-wreathed barges anchored in midstream, crowded with families trying to avoid the bubonic plague. Reminders of the deadly plague were everywhere. The epic *Company of Adventurers* relates that as Radisson and des Groseilliers sailed under London Bridge, "they were given perfumed handkerchiefs to cut the stench of putrefaction coming from the 'plague pits' where victims were dumped."

A series of setbacks beyond their control followed the Frenchmen during their stay in England. First, there was strong anti-French sentiment in England because of accusations that the French were responsible for starting the London fire of 1666. Second, England was at war with the Dutch from 1665 to 1668. During this time, the Dutch fleet sailed right up the Thames River, destroyed the navy line of defence and captured the Royal Navy flagship.

But Radisson and des Groseilliers were promoters *extraordinaire*. They continued to drum up support, saying the right things and connecting with important people. They fuelled rumours that the Hudson Bay Project (as they called it) would make its investors rich and perhaps even lead the way to a long sought-after "northwest passage."

They eventually gained the confidence of the powerful London financiers and courtiers, and even King Charles II himself. Having the king's support moved things ahead rapidly, and by 1668 the French duo were positioned to lead England to the territories north of New France.

The Historic *Nonsuch* Voyage

Two ships were outfitted for the historic journey to the Hudson Bay. The 43-foot ketch (a sailing vessel with two masts) *Nonsuch*, named after an English palace, was commanded

The *Nonsuch* on its maiden voyage

by Captain Zachary Gillam with des Groseilliers on board. The ketch *Eaglet*, commanded by Captain William Stannard, had Radisson on board.

Sailing to the Hudson Bay was not a new adventure for the British. The bay was named for an English explorer and mariner, Henry Hudson, who had entered the bay in 1610 aboard the *Discovery*. However, this voyage had a tragic end. His crew mutinied in 1611 and put Hudson, his 12-year-old son and several crew members adrift in a small boat on the ice-filled bay. They were never seen again.

Others had also sailed the Hudson Bay, but all told of its deprivation and isolation. No one had sailed to the bay for 25 years. It was known as a dangerous and forbidding place. If there was wind, a captain had some control. But if there was no wind, ships could drift along at risk of hitting massive ice floes.

These dangers, however, did not stop Radisson and des Groseilliers. On a misty morning in June 1668, the *Nonsuch* and the *Eaglet* slipped their moorings and sailed from Gravesend, England. They reached the open sea and headed north. After rounding the Orkneys at the far northern tip of Scotland, they headed due west toward the New World. The crew knew it was a hazardous journey, but Radisson and des Groseilliers were confident the mission would be a success.

It did not take long for trouble to strike. Four hundred leagues off Ireland, there was a tremendous storm and Radisson, with the *Eaglet*, was forced to return to Plymouth for repairs. Des Groseilliers, aboard the *Nonsuch*, continued on and reached James Bay in September 1668, three months after their departure from England. The crew carried provisions ashore to a site on the mouth of the river they named Rupert's River in present-day Quebec. The provisions included such diverse items as tar, compasses, medicines, axes, saws, hammers, blunderbusses, muskets, pistols, powder, shot, beef, peas, oatmeal, raisins, prunes, sugar, spice, oil, lemon juice, paper, quills, eel nets, beer and brandy.

A Successful Return

Des Groseilliers' crew cleared the land of spruce trees and built a house of upright logs caulked with moss, and a roof was made from local thatch. They named the house Charles Fort in honour of the king. (It would later be renamed Rupert's House and is now the site of the Cree community of Waskaganish, Quebec.) To survive the long winter, the crew fished the river for pike and killed hundreds of geese and ptarmigans. They also built a cellar to store their beer. The men spent the winter of 1668–69 at Charles Fort. In the spring, almost 300 Cree from James Bay came to trade.

The crew headed home on June 14, 1669, loaded with a cargo of fine beaver pelts. The cargo sold for over £1,375 the following February. However, when all expenses were considered, the voyage had not made a profit. Despite this, the safe return of the *Nonsuch* with the highest quality furs demonstrated that the Hudson Bay Project was feasible. Thus the financial backers in England, led by Prince Rupert, the cousin of King Charles II, were pleased and ready to out-fit further expeditions.

CHAPTER

3

The Early Days of the HBC

ON MAY 2, 1670, KING CHARLES II granted a Royal Charter to the new company, officially known as The Governor and Adventurers Trading into the Hudson Bay. The charter, which was written on five sheepskin parchments with over 7,000 words of handwritten text, stated the new company's three goals: fur trading, mineral exploration and finding a northwest passage.

The document was an astonishing Royal Charter for the new proprietors of what would later be known worldwide as the Hudson's Bay Company. The proprietors included the king's cousin, Prince Rupert, and 17 other business associates. Later, in June, the first woman shareholder, Lady Margaret Drax, the wife of a financier, signed on, increasing the total number of shareholders to 19. Calling them "true lords and proprietors," the king gave the new company sole possession of all the seas, waters, lakes and lands of the Hudson Bay and its drainage system. It was one of the most generous gifts ever given by a king. Although the grant was significant, bestowing land was not unusual for the heads of state in Europe. The chartering of companies by the English crown was an established method of trade and territorial expansion. For example, similar gifts had been granted to slave traders and gold hunters in west Africa.

This real estate windfall in the New World was a virtual subcontinent of 3.8 million square kilometres of land. Geographically, it extended from the unexplored regions of Labrador in the east to the Canadian Rockies in the west. In between, it included the area sandwiched between what is present-day Quebec and Ontario, all of Manitoba, southern Saskatchewan, Alberta and the eastern portion of the Northwest Territories. It also included land south of the 49th parallel, taking in much of Minnesota and North Dakota in today's USA.

In this vast new territory, the company had absolute power to establish and enforce laws and to erect forts, as well as have its own soldiers, maintain a navy and make peace— or war—with the Native peoples. (War with other Christian sovereigns required the permission of the British king.) In effect, the company could run its empire any way it wanted. This land was to be called Rupert's Land, after Prince Rupert, the chief lobbyist for the Company. The area was equivalent to almost 40 percent of modern-day Canada.

The Adventurers Spring Into Action

To Radisson and des Groseilliers, the importance of the Royal Charter was simply "a good transport to more fur trading." After wintering in London in 1670–71, they were restless. These were men of action and time was moving on. A month after the Company was awarded its formal Charter, the two Frenchmen sailed back to the bay. The frigate *Prince Rupert*, commanded by their old friend Captain Gillam, carried des Groseilliers and Thomas Gorst. The *Wivenhoe*, commanded by Captain Newlands, sailed with Radisson and Charles Bayly, the first overseas governor of the new company.

Again, tragedy struck early. After successfully navigating the *Wivenhoe* through the treacherous waters of the Hudson Strait, Newlands died of scurvy. The crew buried him with honour at Charles Fort in October 1670. Captain Newlands was the first European to be buried there. It was a sombre beginning but the expedition continued. The crew's main task was to build a permanent fort on the Nelson River from which Bayly was to govern the entire region for the Hudson's Bay Company. But it didn't happen. They did land on the estuary of the Nelson River, and Bayly did nail the King's Arms to a tree, claiming the territory for England. However, an autumn gale drove the *Wivenhoe* back into deep water and the crew was forced to sail eastward across the bay, a distance of 1,158 kilometres, to join the other ship. Both crews spent the winter at Charles Fort at the lower end of the bay.

There was much work to do during the long, dark winter. A shallop (a small, light, open boat propelled by sail or oars), called the *Royal Charles*, was built to sail goods and people locally. In January, Radisson left on a three-month exploratory expedition to Moose River. And the governor, ever mindful of the death of Captain Newlands, kept the local Native peoples busy hunting fresh meat to ward off scurvy.

From Madman to Governor

Charles Bayly was a fanatical Quaker and a strange choice for the historic first overseas governorship. He came to the position straight out of jail. Some say he came by his position because he was a childhood playmate of King Charles II. His French mother was a lady-in-waiting to Charles' French mother, Henrietta Maria, daughter of Henry IV of France. His father was unknown.

Bayly's early years were filled with adventure. While still in his teens, he was shipped overseas to endure 14 years as a bond servant in the English-American colony of Virginia. While there, he is believed to have met the Quaker missionary, Elizabeth Harris. The Quakers were an early American religious group who protested established church conventions. They were often persecuted for believing each human being could contact God directly. Bayly soon became a convert.

Eventually Bayly returned to Europe and travelled to Rome, where he met up with another Quaker zealot, John Perrot. Their unusual mission was to convert the pope to the Quaker faith. For their efforts, however, both Bayly and Perrot were confined to a madhouse, where Bayly fasted in protest for 20 days. They were then thrown out of Italy. In defiance, Bayly walked barefoot across France. He was often arrested and jailed before finally returning to England.

The more temperate Quakers excommunicated Bayly for his eccentricity. In England, he also ended up in various dungeons and prisons, where he wrote letters to his boyhood friend, King Charles II. Sometimes the letters would warn the king to change his ways or "be threatened with a share in the whirlwind of the Lord." King Charles confined him to the Tower of London from 1663 to 1669. Most thought he was insane and he became known as "an old Quaker with a long beard."

Then a strange thing happened. In 1669, the king released Bayly from the tower—on condition that he "betook himself to the navigation of Hudson Bay and the places lately discovered and to be discovered in those parts." So Bayly, the religious fanatic, became the first overseas governor of the Hudson's Bay Company. For the next nine years, he did an admirable job of conducting business. He established posts at the estuaries of the major rivers flowing into the James and Hudson bays. He founded a supply depot on Charlton Island in James Bay and planned the HBC's factory system. He traded fairly with the Native peoples and became an astute businessman.

The HBC's First Auction

In 1671, the HBC ships left the bay laden with a rich harvest of fur and arrived back in London in October. The Company decided to sell the pelts in two fur auctions at Garraway's Coffee House near the Royal Exchange in London. The first HBC sale was posted for January 24, 1672. Garraway's was famous for introducing tea to England in 1651. Some of the country's most influential citizens socialized at the coffee house. It was a logical place to sell furs and make lots of money.

The bidding was done by candle, a somewhat odd bidding procedure that occurred in one of two ways. One bidding procedure required that a one-inch candle be lit and bids made. When the candle guttered out, the highest bidder secured the goods. Another procedure was that a pin was stuck into the tallow of a candle and a purchaser (the highest bidder) was declared when the pin fell out. Bidding at Garraway's was a noisy gala drawing the elite of English society. Prince Rupert was there, as was his cousin, the Duke of York. A Restoration poet named John Dryden later captured the evening in verse:

Friend, once 'twas Fame that led thee forth,
To brave the tropic heat, the frozen North,
Later 'twas gold. Then beauty was the spur,
But now our gallants venture but for fur.

Radisson and des Groseilliers Leave the HBC

The HBC's 1672 expedition arrived at Charles Fort in September. Under Bayly, the fort carried out business as usual, but seething tensions were developing between Bayly and Radisson and des Groseilliers. So intense was the distrust, it led to the dramatic departure of the two Frenchmen from the fur-trading empire they had helped found. It wasn't a secret that Bayly disliked the two Frenchmen. He constantly reminded them that he was the governor, and he knowingly irritated them by closely watching their activities. The situation was ripe for confrontation.

In the early winter of 1672–73, the Native people around Charles Fort became noticeably more wary of the English. They had met with Frenchmen in the area who had told them the English were not to be trusted and that their guns were bewitched and their religion evil. Governor Bayly became worried the Natives were contemplating an attack on Charles Fort. He immediately began the task of strengthening the fort's defences.

Surprisingly, the winter passed without incident, until March, when six Native ambassadors came to the fort to announce that their chief, Kas-Kidi-dah (also called King

Cusciddidah in the HBC records), would soon be arriving. When the chief arrived the next day, Gorst, who was acting as recorder, reported, "His Majestie brought a retinue with him but very little beaver, the Indians haveing already sent their best to Canada." But both the governor and Radisson were absent from the fort that day. They were out hunting together, but not out of comraderie. Bayly had privately sworn that he would never trust Radisson at the fort without him—so they went together on all expeditions outside the fort.

In Bayly's absence, Captain Cole was in charge. Cole panicked in the presence of so many Native people tenting around the fort. Under cover of darkness, he sent two men to look for the governor. Chief Kas-Kidi-dah also sent two of his men to look for Bayly.

When the governor returned, however, Radisson was not with him. No explanation was offered. The next day a rumour circulated that Bayly and Radisson had quarrelled in the wilderness. The argument led to blows and finally—so the rumour went—Radisson had attempted to shoot Bayly.

Des Groseilliers was alarmed and tried to find out the true story. But Bayly would neither confirm nor deny the rumour. It wasn't until des Groseilliers met with Chief Kas-Kidi-dah in the chief's *wigwam* that he learned the whereabouts of his partner. The chief told him about a French post on the banks of the Moose River, an eight-day journey from Rupert's River. He said Radisson had headed there and was planning to make his way back to New France. Some stories persist, however, that Radisson returned to the bay and in September sailed back to England on the HBC ship. Regardless, Radisson was gone by the fall.

Des Groseilliers and Bayly stayed another winter, but tensions continued. Des Groseilliers began to suspect that Bayly had been trying to drive both him and Radisson out of the HBC all along.

In early April 1674, there was talk of a raid on the fort by hostile Native peoples in the area. Bayly, des Groseilliers and Cole held a council to decide how to protect themselves against such an attack. They opted to head for the Moose River once all of the Native peoples, friend or foe, had left the region to hunt. It wasn't until the end of May that the HBC men could head out. At the last moment, however, Bayly said he wasn't going, and remained at Charles Fort.

Soon after the group arrived at the mouth of the Moose River, a band of Tahiti Indians came to trade 200 beaver pelts. During the trading ceremony, the chief of the Tahitis stared intently at des Groseilliers and then—suddenly— broke off the discussions. When Cole asked why, the chief said he recognized des Groseilliers as a Frenchman with whom he had dealt many years ago. Des Groseilliers admitted they had met before, but told the chief not to be alarmed. He was trading as an "Englishman" with the HBC, and not as an independent *coureur du bois*. The chief remained hostile. He reminded des Groseilliers, "You drove hard bargains. You took our silkiest, softest, and richest furs, and you gave us but beads and ribbons."

Des Groseilliers, a veteran fur trader, was not concerned by the charges. He was experienced in trade negotiations with Native peoples. He knew how to play to the situation, to defuse the moment. He politely reiterated his position, and trading continued. The damage, however, had been done.

When they returned to the fort, Bayly was told the Tahitis had refused to deal with des Groseilliers. Bayly decided to investigate. He arrived at Moose River at the same time as a nation from Albany who had come to trade with him. He traded over 1,500 beaver pelts. Later, as he travelled along the coast, he met other Native groups and they reassured him they would take their furs to the HBC instead of to the French.

Bayly returned to Charles Fort in July to find it in chaos. Des Groseilliers and Gorst were fighting—and the HBC staff was close to mutiny—all because they objected to serving under a Frenchman.

As if things weren't tense enough, a few days later a Jesuit priest, Father Albanel, arrived by canoe at the fort. Father Albanel presented Bayly with a letter from Governor Talon in Quebec. Bayly was thrilled with the letter, a communication, Talon said, "from one great man to another." The letter, which Bayly read publicly at the fort, asked Bayly to treat Father Albanel with politeness. Bayly did so.

However, later that evening, the governor learned that the Jesuit priest had also delivered letters to des Groseilliers. Bayly was convinced of treachery, and that the visit by Father Albanel was a ruse to capture the fort and let it be pillaged by hostile Indians. He ordered des Groseilliers brought to him. When Gorst told him that the Jesuit priest and des Groseilliers were walking and chatting, he went out and found the pair himself. Bayly confronted des Groseilliers, yelling and screaming accusations at him. Finally, des Groseilliers had had enough. He knocked the governor down. Apparently, des Groseilliers returned calmly to the fort, took his possessions and wages and, together with four companions, set off on an overland journey to Quebec.

By December 1675, both Radisson and des Groseilliers had officially severed their ties with the HBC. Des Groseilliers resumed life at Trois-Rivières in Quebec. Radisson sailed with the French navy until he was shipwrecked in 1679. He then made his way to Paris and on to England, where he visited his wife, Mary Kirke, the daughter of adventurer Sir John Kirke, one of the original 18 investors of the HBC.

But the departure of Radisson and des Groseilliers from the fur trade was just an interlude. The HBC and its two founding fur traders still had more adventures to come.

CHAPTER

4

Standoff

THE WINTER OF 1682–83 ON the bay was one of the strang-
est in the history of fur trading. A bizarre set of events
led to some unexpected drama. It began in August 1682
when two decrepit French sloops arrived at the estuary
of the Nelson and Hayes Rivers. Their sea journey had
been difficult, with two attempted mutinies, rough water
and dangerous ice conditions. Once the vessels reached
Hayes River, they proceeded 24 kilometres upstream and
established a fur-trading post. The 50-ton *St. Pierre* had a
crew of 12, and the smaller sloop *St. Anne* carried 15 men.
Their commanders were none other than the famous fur-
trading soldiers of fortune, Radisson and des Groseilliers.
This time, however, they were representing La Compagnie

du Nord, a rival French fur-trading company they had recently started with partners from New France.

On the south side of Hayes River, the crews had begun constructing a fort which they named Fort Bourbon. Radisson had taken a canoe to explore further upstream and made contact with some Native hunters. Along with him were des Groseilliers' 27-year-old son, Jean-Baptiste, and a veteran bush ranger. They returned on September 12 and were back for only a short time when, suddenly, they heard the sound of a distant cannon.

The New Englanders

Radisson and des Groseilliers were disturbed when they realized that someone else was sailing in this remote area of the world. Radisson quickly canoed to the mouth of the river to investigate. He located a tent on a small island in the Nelson River and saw a group of men building a log house in the distance.

The next morning, Radisson paddled towards the camp. He was careful to stay some distance from the shore. Radisson hailed the men, speaking first in French, then English. He asked what they were doing here. They called back, "We are English and come for the beaver trade," adding that they came from New England. Radisson told them they had no right to be there, saying that some years ago he discovered and claimed the area for the French. He told them to leave.

As Radisson was talking, the canoe of Frenchmen

drifted close to shore. There was an unexpected silence. Then—a loud cry of surprise—Radisson recognized the leader. It was Benjamin Gillam, the youngest son of his old friend Captain Zachary Gillam. They embraced warmly, though Radisson, ever prudent, remained cautious. Gillam invited Radisson on his ship, the *Bachelor's Delight*. The Frenchman accepted, but kept two of Gillam's crew on shore as hostages.

The meeting was cordial. Radisson bluffed Gillam with claims of massive French forces on the river and "absolute power" over the Native peoples. He gave Gillam permission to stay the winter, as it was too late in the season to safely sail out. And he allowed him to continue building the log fort, but insisted it not be fortified. They parted on relatively friendly terms.

The French party returned to their canoe and headed back. Young Gillam's unexpected presence complicated matters for the Frenchmen, but Radisson felt he had matters under control. However, the events unfolding on the two rivers were about to get more complicated.

The HBC Returns to the Nelson River
On September 7, as Radisson paddled northward, another surprise unfolded. He spotted a Hudson's Bay Company ship heading up the Nelson River. Quickly, the French party went ashore and started a huge bonfire. Thick columns of smoke rose in the air. The HBC crew saw the smoke and dropped

anchor for the night, thinking the smoke was from a Native encampment.

Captain Zachary Gillam navigated his HBC ship, the *Prince Rupert*, into the mouth of the Nelson River. He had been there before, in 1670. Sailing with him at that time had been Radisson and the HBC's first overseas governor, Charles Bayly. It had been their intent to establish a main HBC post on the Nelson River, but the attempt had failed. Now, 12 years later, Gillam was back to complete the task with another HBC man, John Bridgar, the governor for the new fort which would be called Port Nelson.

The senior Gillam was probably aware that his 20-year-old son, sea captain and adventurer Benjamin Gillam, and 14 New Englanders would be there that winter on the Hudson Bay. Benjamin had secured licences from the governor of Massachusetts to trade furs in the area.

Zachary Gillam had almost missed this voyage. His career with the HBC had been a rocky one. The HBC had fired him nine years before for private trading. He had returned to New England to carry on coastal trading. He had recently been hired back by the HBC, and in March he got back command of his old ship, the *Prince Rupert*. But by May, he had risked dismissal again after being charged with misconduct (this time he had been absent during his ship's loading).

Nevertheless, in June, he was at the helm of the *Prince Rupert* once more. Five ships had been sent by the Hudson's Bay Company to the area that year. Two of these, the *Prince*

Rupert and the *Albercome*, were directed to proceed to the Nelson and Hayes Rivers to establish Port Nelson. Only Gillam's ship arrived.

Old Friends Meet Again

The next morning, Radisson was armed and ready when the HBC ship sent a boat to investigate. The master of bluff was about to go to work again. He strode out to the shore to greet the strangers. As the boat neared, he bellowed out in a loud voice in English, "Hold, in the king's name. I forbid you to land." He showed his gun. Astonished, the group's leader, HBC governor Bridgar, told him they were Englishmen. He asked him who he was and what business he had in stopping them. Radisson replied defiantly in English, "I am a Frenchman and I hold this country for this Most Christian Majesty, King Louis!" In a show of force, the other two Frenchmen in his party dramatically emerged from the woods, brandishing their weapons.

Bridgar, standing up in his boat, announced, "I beg to inform you, gentlemen, that we hail from London. Our ship yonder is the *Prince Rupert*, belonging to the honourable Hudson's Bay Company and commanded by Captain Zachary Gillam."

"You arrive too late," yelled Radisson. "This country is already in the possession of the King of France."

A short verbal dispute arose, as both Bridgar and Radisson claimed jurisdiction. Bridgar invited Radisson to continue the discussion on board the *Prince Rupert*. Radisson accepted, but as before, his men held two Englishmen on shore as hostages.

Captain Zachary Gillam embraced Radisson. Their relationship went back 20 years to when the two Frenchmen were first looking for investors in New England. Radisson and his brother-in-law had successfully captured Gillam's interest in their project of a fur-trading venture in the Hudson Bay area. Now, however, neither of the men trusted the other. And each of them had made serious charges against the other before leaving the Hudson's Bay Company.

During their shipboard conversation, Radisson bragged to Bridgar and the senior Gillam that he had two ships in the vicinity, was expecting a third French ship any day and was building a huge fort. Bridgar listened intently and pretended to be impressed. But after Radisson left, he ignored the threats of the Frenchman and sent his men on shore to build Port Nelson, on the north side of the Nelson River.

However, the fall brought more complications for the English. Autumn gales on the Hudson Bay were known for their severity, and on October 21, 1682, there was a ferocious storm. High winds whipped up huge waves and the strong currents made the seas dangerous and deadly. During this storm, the *Prince Rupert*'s anchor came loose, and the ship was blown out to sea and sank. Radisson and des Groseilliers' old friend Captain Zachary Gillam drowned, along with several crew members.

A Challenging Winter

Radisson and des Groseilliers knew they could not defeat their rivals with a show of force. Instead, they used their superior trade experience and bush knowledge to operate more effectively than their rivals. They continued to control the situation, while making significant fur profits. Des Groseilliers and his son carried out the fur trading, while Radisson spied and managed the two groups of English. To monitor their activities, Radisson travelled between the three forts, sometimes putting himself in great danger. Radisson describes returning from Gillam's fort after a tremendous blizzard.

"On leaving we went up from the fort to the upper part of the river, but in the evening we retraced our steps and next morning found ourselves in sight of the sea into which it was necessary to enter in order to pass the point and reach the river in which was our habitation. But everything was so covered with ice that there was no apparent way of passing further. We found ourselves, indeed, so entangled in the ice that we could neither retreat nor advance towards the shore to make a landing.

"It was necessary, however, that we should pass through the ice or perish. We remained in this condition for four hours without being able to advance or retire, and in great danger of our lives. Our clothes were frozen on us and we could only move with difficulty, but at last we made so strong an attempt that we arrived at the shore, our canoe being all broken up. Each of us took our baggage and arms and marched into [sic] the direction of our habitation, without finding anything to eat for three days except crows and birds of prey . . . "

Radisson maintained control of the area by outwitting the HBC men and the New Englanders. When he thought the New Englanders were defying his authority, he invited the junior Gillam for a month's visit at the French fort, then took him prisoner.

He wrote, "I remained quiet for a month treating young Gillam, my new guest, well and with all sorts of civilities, which he abused on several occasions. For having apparently perceived that we had not the strength I told him, he took the liberty of speaking of me in threatening terms behind my back, treating me as a pirate and saying that, in spite of me, he would trade in spring with the Indians. He had even the hardihood to strike one of my men which I pretended not to notice. He left me, threatening that he would return to his fort . . . I told this young brute then that I had brought him from his fort, that I would take him back myself, when I pleased, not when he wished." With Gillam now as his prisoner, Radisson and nine of his men went to Gillam's fort. Without encountering any resistance, they seized Gillam's fort and his ship.

Finally, in the summer of 1683, Radisson took control of the HBC's Port Nelson. After learning that Governor

Bridgar had planned a night attack on Fort Bourbon (Radisson's own fort), Radisson turned the tables on the governor and marched to Port Nelson with 12 men, seizing the fort. He then took the unhappy governor back to Fort Bourbon as a prisoner.

Living on the Edge

After the seizure of the forts and pelts, as well as the HBC men and the New Englanders, the Frenchmen's priority was to sell their furs to European customers. They also needed to transport their prisoners, Bridgar, young Gillam and the New Englanders, to New France. The other prisoners were allowed to return to their HBC posts on James Bay. But the endeavour, once again, did not go according to plan.

During spring breakup, their two French sloops were destroyed. Eventually, they constructed one sloop out of the two shipwrecks. Then, on July 27, soon after the ships departed from the Nelson River, the *Bachelor's Delight* became jammed in the ice of the Hudson Bay. The sloop, which was sailing alongside it, split open. "We remained in this perilous position surrounded by ice floes until August 24," wrote Radisson.

Finally, in October, the *Bachelor's Delight* reached its destination only to find another unpleasant surprise. The French tax collector was waiting for them. He levied a 25 percent duty on the furs and confiscated the ship. Again, New France was tampering with the profits of Radisson and des Groseilliers, profits that they had gained partly at the expense of their new rival, the HBC. But the Hudson's Bay Company and its two founding adventurers were not finished with each other quite yet. Amazingly—within a year—the HBC offered to rehire both des Groseilliers and Radisson.

Des Groseilliers declined and returned to domestic life, but Radisson accepted and became the superintendent and director of trade. The following year he returned to the Hudson Bay, bringing back over 20,000 beaver pelts for the HBC. His last voyage in 1687 was short and he kept a low profile. His life was at risk for being a traitor to France, and French commandos were looking for him in the bay.

CHAPTER

5

The Commando Raids

BY ACCEPTING THE HBC'S EMPLOYMENT, Radisson deeply offended the inhabitants of New France. In 1685, the citizens burnt an effigy of Radisson and des Groseilliers, and a decree was issued for their arrest.

The associates of La Compagnie du Nord (the fur-trading company Radisson helped start in 1682 to challenge HBC) were also infuriated by Radisson's rekindled allegiance with the Hudson's Bay Company. They demanded swift military action from the governor of New France, Jacques-René de Brisay, Marquis de Denonville—and got it.

The Expedition
De Brisay ordered a military expedition that had two goals.

The first was to drive the English out of the northern bays and the second was to capture the HBC forts. The governor appointed a veteran French officer, Chevalier Pierre de Troyes, as the unit's commander. De Troyes had come to New France only eight months prior, as the captain of the colony's marines. A brave officer and a strict disciplinarian, he was said to be a good planner and improviser, and to have "wit and prudence." Some said he was looking for an opportunity to become a hero, to make his mark in history.

The governor gave de Troyes a wide mandate. He empowered him to "search for, seize and occupy the most advantageous posts, to seize the robbers, bush rangers, and others . . . we order him to arrest, especially the said Radisson and his adherents wherever they may be found, and bring them to be punished as deserters, according to the rigour of the ordinances." The penalty for desertion was death.

De Troyes assembled a small but strong military unit of 107 men: 30 French soldiers (*Troupes de la Marine*), 70 Canadian irregulars, six native guides and one Jesuit priest, Father Sylvie. De Troyes' lieutenants were three brothers who grew up in the area of the fur trade and were expert bush rangers. The eldest was 25-year-old Pierre Le Moyne d'Iberville, who would later become one of Canada's most famous naval commanders. The other two were Paul Le Moyne de Maricourt and Jacques Le Moyne de Sainte-Hélène (as was the custom, their last names were taken from places in France).

The commando unit left Montreal on March 3, 1686, after attending Mass at the Church of Notre Dame. It was a surreal departure, a rag-tag army tramping northward on snowshoes along the frozen Ottawa River, dragging behind them sleds and 35 canoes. The trip was an epic overland journey, over 1,200 kilometres of virgin territory. North up the Ottawa River and the Mattawa River to Lake Temiskami. Along the White River to the Abitibi River and Lake Abitibi. North on the Moose River to James Bay, where the HBC forts were located.

It was a gruelling trek. No large expeditions had travelled this way to the northern bays. The men had to deal with the many dangers of the spring breakup. They detoured around ice, cut portage pathways, struggled overland, navigated rapids, and recovered and repaired capsized canoes. They stumbled over rotten logs, fallen trees, slippery rocks and dense underbrush. And near the end of the journey, they fought large hordes of black flies.

On June 19, 82 days after leaving Montreal, the commando unit was near the first HBC fort, Moose Factory. Chevalier de Troyes wasted no time. After a reconnaissance mission, he located the fort on a large island in the Moose River and decided to attack the next day. The troop constructed a battering ram and sharpened the blades of their swords.

All the while, the Cree watched the Frenchmen. They were angry at the treatment they received from the local Hudson's Bay Company. As the French troops prepared for assault, the Cree remained silent. When the attackers slowly crept close and quietly surrounded the fort, the Cree did not sound an alarm. They continued to watch from the sidelines.

Attack on Moose Factory

In the darkness of night, the Frenchmen surrounded the wooden log palisade of Moose Factory. It was 5.5 metres high and protected by a cannon at each corner. In the centre of the fort was a three-storey building armed with four cannons. Access to the fort was through the large main entrance doors at the front, with a small sally port at the rear. Inside the fort, 16 leaderless men were sleeping in their quarters. Their leader, Governor John Bridgar, had left the day before to sail to Charles Fort, along with most of the officers. The attack was led by two of the brothers, Pierre d'Iberville and Jacques de Sainte-Hélène. While the HBC men slept, they tiptoed inside to rope the cannons together and then slipped out again.

De Troyes positioned his men strategically. Rough ladders were placed to scale the walls, then they were ready for battle. De Troyes gave the word to attack and the stillness of night was shattered. The commandos shouted the war whoop of the Iroquois as they swarmed over the walls and through the front door. A chief gunner bravely fought from his post, but d'Iberville killed him by splitting open his head. The rest of the stunned HBC men put up little resistance. They were Company servants, not soldiers. They surrendered. The battle took only half an hour.

"I had discovered that I had great difficulty," Chevalier de Troyes wrote later, "trying to stop the assault of the Canadians, who, screaming like savages, demanding [sic] the opportunity to use their knives."

Nearby, the commando troops recaptured one of their old sailing ships, *La Sainte-Anne,* which had previously been seized by the Hudson's Bay Company and renamed *St. Anne.* The ship became a holding cell for the HBC prisoners. Forty Frenchmen were left to guard Moose Factory.

Attack on Charles Fort

The commandos moved on toward Charles Fort, 120 kilometres from Moose Factory, along the east coast of James Bay. De Sainte-Hélène was in charge of the scouting mission. He returned on July 2, saying the way was clear for their second attack. The troops, led by Pierre d'Iberville, headed out in birchbark war canoes and sighted the fort. Nearby, lying at anchor was the HBC ship, the *Craven.* The attack came at night, and without much of a fight the troops captured Charles Fort.

While the land assault was going on, d'Iberville silently boarded the *Craven.* Swiftly, he killed a dozing HBC sailor at anchor watch. Then, to wake up the crew and get them to scramble to the deck, he stamped his feet, a traditional mariner's emergency signal. Crew members raced up the companionway and three Englishmen were killed by the blunt end of d'Iberville's musket. The rest quickly surrendered.

All the prisoners, including the hapless Governor Bridgar, were taken back to Moose Factory. For the second time in four years Bridgar was a prisoner of the French. Charles Fort was ransacked and the furniture and valuables loaded on the *Craven*. The fort was destroyed.

Pierre d'Iberville sailed the *Craven* to Moose Factory and readied the ship for an assault on the more heavily armed Fort Albany, at the mouth of the Albany River.

Attack on Fort Albany

Back at Moose Factory, de Troyes and his commanders planned their raid on Fort Albany (975 kilometres from Montreal). It was the most protected of the Hudson Bay forts, with 43 guns, log walls and four cannon bastions. In mid-July, the French commandos headed out, transporting troops and equipment on the two captured ships, the *La Sainte-Anne* and the *Craven*. But locating Fort Albany was not an easy task. Situated on the bay's west coast, on a sheltered inlet a short distance up the Albany River, Fort Albany was not visible from the water. This became a tricky problem for the French. They were ready to attack, but couldn't find the fort.

However, just as they were ready to abandon the search, the English fired their daily sunset salute—and immediately gave away their location. De Troyes and d'Iberville set to work. The heavy siege guns, captured from Charles Fort, were mounted on the frozen gravel outside the fort's palisade. Then 140 shots were fired.

Governor Sergeant of Fort Albany was sitting down to a glass of wine with supper when the attack started. Some say the governor had expected the French. Hours before he had been warned by two Natives of an impending attack. They had told him that both Moose Factory and Charles Fort had fallen. He prepared Fort Albany to stand a siege and encouraged everyone to be brave.

The bombardment continued for two days. Occasionally, the English responded with cannon fire. The first fatality occurred on the evening of the second day, when an HBC servant was killed. The HBC men were terrified. Sergeant overheard his chief gunner, Elias Turner, tell his comrades that he wanted to surrender to the mercy of the French. Fearing mutiny, Governor Sergeant drew his pistol and threatened to kill Turner if he abandoned his post.

The French used the darkness to take their cannon closer to the fort. A series of heavy balls struck the bastions. At one point, the French were heard shouting, "*Vive le Roi, vive le Roi*" (long live the king). The frightened English repeated the shout, thinking it would appease their attackers. But the French thought it was a shout of defiance and stepped up the gunfire.

Both the French and the English knew that the fort's isolation meant that no reinforcements were possible for either side. No extra food, supplies or munitions would be arriving. Finally, the resident HBC chaplain came through the gate carrying a white flag (some say it was a maid's white apron tied to a walking stick). He arranged for Governor Sergeant to meet with de Troyes.

The surrender meeting was somewhat comical. Sergeant requested that de Troyes meet and talk with him in the middle of the Albany River. Their two small boats set out, one from each riverbank. Sergeant was concerned about the etiquette of the occasion, so had a bottle of good Spanish wine tucked under his arm. As they met in the middle of the river, Sergeant suggested the two leaders drink a toast to their respective sovereigns. They did so.

Meanwhile, de Troyes tried hard to maintain the illusion of power and a strong force, hoping the governor wouldn't notice the vulnerable condition of his men. The long journey from Montreal and three successive raids had taken their toll. The men were hungry and exhausted and could easily have been overrun. But Sergeant was too concerned about saving himself and his family and did not notice their condition. The two leaders negotiated the terms of the English surrender.

Sergeant agreed to surrender the fort the next morning, July 26. Under the surrender terms, he kept his personal possessions, sidearms, swords and his staff (three domestics and a servant). Everyone would be shipped to Charlton Island to wait for the arrival of the fall supply ship from England. De Troyes was disappointed that Radisson was not at the fort. To keep the prisoners from starving, de Troyes promised to provide provisions until the HBC ship arrived.

Three Decades of Conflict

It was an extraordinary wilderness military campaign. None of the French under de Troyes had ever been in that part of the country before. It was all strange new terrain. They did not know the geographical layout nor the travel routes. But it had taken them only 35 days from the time they arrived at James Bay to capture three HBC forts: Moose Factory, Charles Fort and Fort Albany. The French held these three forts until 1693.

At each seized post, de Troyes pompously waved his sword, making speeches of conquest and proclaiming victory in the name of the King of France. And Father Silvie, the Jesuit priest travelling with de Troyes, said prayers for the dead.

D'Iberville and 40 Frenchmen stayed the winter to guard the forts while de Troyes returned to a hero's welcome in Montreal. Denonville, the governor of New France, gushed in conversation: "The sieur de Troyes is the smartest and the most capable of our captains. He has the kind of spirit needed to command others. There can be no better example than the behaviour he demonstrated during our northern undertaking where he needed to be very clever . . . "

D'Iberville returned to the bay the following summer to bring out the captured furs. France appointed the young man commander-in-chief of Hudson Bay for the French. He was not even 30 years of age.

The successful commando raids of 1686 were the beginning of 27 years of undeclared warfare as the French and English tried to remove each other from the Hudson Bay. The northern forts were regularly captured, lost and recaptured. It wasn't until 1713, under the terms of the Treaty of Utrecht, that the HBC regained control of all of its northern forts, and the northern bays—the Hudson Bay and James Bay—again became the exclusive trading domain of the HBC.

6

Remarkable Adventurers of the HBC

THERE ARE MANY REMARKABLE MEN and women who contributed to the colourful history of the Hudson's Bay Company. These are but a few of the adventurers whose lives provide fascinating vignettes of the fur trade in northern Canada.

Prince Rupert

In 1642, King Charles I of England had just appointed his nephew, Prince Rupert (1619–1685), as his "general of hope," a command position independent of any royal or political structure. The king was losing the Civil War and desperately needed Rupert to bring life back to his disorganized military.

Rupert was only 22 years old but he relished the challenge. As a warrior prince, he thrived on adventure and intrigue. Riding his Barbary horse, he led cavalry charges against the king's enemies and won every battle. His daring exploits became legendary. Rupert had a romantic, almost mythical persona that exuded bravado. While riding his horse, he would wear flamboyant clothing. One outfit he wore was a stunning scarlet velvet tunic, embellished with silver lace, topped by a feathered French beaver hat. He was a model of fashion. When he tied a lace handkerchief around his neck other soldiers copied his style. There was a somewhat magical aura around him.

His uncle, King Charles I, adored Rupert and gave him even more power and prestige when he appointed him as his commander-in-chief. Rupert was a military genius, a brilliant strategist. As a seventeenth century military commander, he developed tactics to suddenly and quickly strike the enemy. He valued intelligence gathering and didn't hesitate to put himself on the front line. He once disguised himself as a cabbage vendor and drove a cart into the town of Warwick to gather information about the enemy's defences and troop deployment.

Eventually, his spontaneous strategies failed. When Bristol came under siege, he buckled and surrendered the city in only four days. He lamented, "I have no stomach for sieges." He was accused of cowardice and court martialled for betrayal, but was cleared of any "lack of courage."

King Charles I lost the war and was beheaded in 1649. Rupert's military career appeared to be over. However, he was about to begin an exciting new phase of military life. After leaving England and briefly joining the French army, Rupert took to the high seas as a daring royal buccaneer. With his flagship, the *Reformation*, and a small armada, he raided galleons and seized goods for the treasury of his royal cousin, the now-exiled Charles II, the son of King Charles I. As a swashbuckling privateer, Prince Rupert roamed the Atlantic Ocean, from the shores of Africa to the Caribbean's West Indies.

His name struck terror on the waters until one day—in a hurricane off the Azores—tragedy struck his fleet. A violent storm had blown in, wreaking deadly havoc on every ship caught in the water. It was a seaman's nightmare. Rupert's entire fleet was lost to the sea. Over 360 crew members perished on the *Reformation*. Somehow, Rupert and twelve others, including his brother Maurice, escaped death. They even saved a portion of the treasure.

After this ordeal, rather than return to his life of privateering on the high seas, Rupert became a mercenary, a soldier of fortune, for the King of Hungary.

When King Charles II was restored to power in 1660, so was Rupert. For his past service to royalty, Rupert garnered a lifetime annual pension of £1,500. He was named admiral of the British Fleet and secured the powerful office of first lord of the admiralty. Rupert was a superb naval commander in fighting the Dutch and in restoring discipline to the Royal Navy.

He never married, but he did father two children, a daughter, Ruperta (whose mother was a beautiful actress named Margaret "Peg" Hughes) and a son, Dudley (whose mother, Francesca Bard, was the daughter of an Irish peer).

Rupert lived an incredible and fast-paced life of adventure. However, in his forties, Rupert took a different and much more serious direction in life. In his last 15 years he achieved an amazing number of accomplishments and creations. This aging warrior became an outstanding philosopher, scientist, artist, inventor and metallurgist. His world revolved around his books, art, poodles (he taught one of his dogs to jump at the word "Charles") and his private laboratory and metal forge at Windsor Castle. His business interests included investing in diversified commercial ventures.

Peter C. Newman writes, "He is credited with fashioning the first primitive torpedo; the forerunners of the modern revolver and machine gun; a new method of manufacturing hail-shot; a useful new alloy of copper and zinc still called 'Prince's Metal'; the tear-shaped glass globules known as 'Rupert's Drops' that led to the making of bulletproof glass; a new means of boring cannon to ensure truer aim; a naval quadrant making it possible to take observations at sea in rough weather; and a 'diving engine' successfully used to retrieve pieces-of-eight from the sunken Spanish treasure ship *Nuestra Senora de la Concepcion*."

When Rupert was faced with brain surgery in 1667 to ease his migraines, he designed and forged the surgical instruments to be used in the operation.

In addition, Prince Rupert, warrior and scientist, also became involved in the fur trade in the New World. It was the lure of profit that drew Rupert to meet with the French trader-adventurers, Radisson and des Groseilliers, in London. He listened intently to their detailed business plan to trade furs in the subarctic of North America using ocean-going vessels sailing to the northern bays. He was entranced with stories of their wilderness experiences and impressed with their cosmopolitan manner, surprised they fit so easily into European society. He admired their aggressive marketing and their determination to set up a lucrative fur trade in the Hudson and James bays. Radisson and des Groseilliers were offering investors an opportunity to make huge profits. They needed risk takers to fund the first exploratory voyage to Hudson Bay. They needed Prince Rupert to buy into the project. And he did.

A man of action, he wasted no time organizing a private syndicate of his business associates to fund the initial expedition. Rupert enlisted a group of risk-taking men, and one woman (a month after the syndicate was formed), who wanted to get very rich, very quickly, as did Radisson and des Groseilliers.

Later, when King Charles II signed a Royal Charter for the project, Rupert, the remarkable man of diverse talents, became the chief executive officer of the Hudson's Bay Company. As the company's overall governor, he was the head of one of the largest corporations in the world. The soldier had become the corporate man.

When Rupert died quietly in 1683, at 64 years of age, he was the head of a fur-trading empire in a vast land—named Rupert's Land in his honour—a territory covering over 40 percent of today's Canada.

Governor James Knight

Some of the HBC men called Governor James Knight "Gold-finders," saying he had gold fever. The older he got, the more obsessed he became with finding the "yellow metal" in the northern lands. Until it killed him.

Knight's career with the HBC spanned 46 years. He joined the Company as a carpenter in 1676, building and repairing the factories at Moose, Rupert and Albany Rivers. He rose quickly in the corporate ranks to become chief factor at Fort Albany and then deputy governor of the bay.

In 1687, Knight left the HBC after being charged with private trading, the most serious charge against an HBC employee. Five years later, the HBC lured him back and made him the governor and commander-in-chief of all forts, factories and territories in Hudson Bay. At the time, the battle in the bays between the English and the French was intense. Forts were lost, recaptured and lost again. The 1713 Treaty of Utrecht returned all the forts to the Hudson's Bay Company.

Knight, at almost 75 years of age, arrived at York Factory with his deputy, Henry Kelsey, on September 5, 1714. A few weeks later, a remarkable woman, Thanadelthur, whom Knight called "the slave woman," came into his life. She brought peace to her people, the Chipewyan, and helped to expand the fur trade into new areas of the far north. Thanadelthur was a valuable source of advice and information for James Knight.

Her stories of yellow metal stirred the merchant adventurer in him. Day after day, he questioned her and other Chipewyan about the northern lands. About "virgin copper lumps . . . so big that three or four men can't lift [them]." About yellow metal used by Native peoples of the west seas. So enthralled was Knight about the potential of wealth from minerals that he added silver and pearls to his quest for mines. He constantly talked about the gold and minerals with Thanadelthur. She told him stories about seeing and handling the yellow metal that came from islands off the west coast. She promised Knight she would go with her brother to get the gold, but she died before the journey could be made. Knight's only source of geographical information about what lay beyond was the Native people.

A year after Thanadelthur's death, Knight was back in England with one goal in mind—to get the HBC Committee to fund his expedition to find a northwest passage, so that he could find the gold and other valuable commodities to the northwest. He succeeded. On June 4, 1719, Knight sailed from

Gravenhurst with two ships: a frigate, the *Albany*, under Captain George Berley; and a sloop, the *Discovery*, under Captain David Vaughan. Cargo included trading goods (blankets, knives, mirrors, beads and muskets) and large quantities of building materials, including brick and lime. They also carried provisions for about nine months, including a large amount of salt for preserving the fresh meat Knight expected to find west of Hudson Bay. And—it was rumoured—the cargo included "large iron-bound chests in which to bring back gold."

The entire expedition was under the control of Knight, who was then around 80 years of age. No expedition details were given to either Captain Berley of the *Albany* nor Captain Vaughan of the *Discovery*. Oddly, the expedition was instructed by the HBC Committee to neither touch at any HBC post nor to sail south into the Hudson Bay unless it was to save their lives. And if this happened, Knight was to put himself under the orders of his successor at York Factory, Henry Kelsey. As the two men disliked each other, perhaps the HBC was attempting to prevent an open clash between two strong leaders. Knight and Kelsey were the only Hudson Bay governors to receive the title of Governor-in-Chief of the Territory of the Company of Adventurers of England trading into Hudson Bay.

The ship's crew headed directly north of 64 degrees, to their deaths on a desolate rock island in the Arctic. No one in the Hudson's Bay Company ever saw or heard from the

Knight expedition's crew again. Two years later, in 1721, Kelsey found evidence among the Inuit that the ships had been wrecked. But he did not pursue an investigation. The following year, Captain John Scroggs of the sloop *Whalebone* reported that the expedition had been destroyed and all the men killed by the Inuit. Subsequently, the HBC wrote off the two ships as lost without ever sending out a search party.

It wasn't until almost 50 years later that the tragic fate of the Knight expedition became known. In 1767, the HBC whaling sloop, the *Success*, anchored at Marble Island. The crew was searching for driftwood when they found a smith's anvil, cannon and shot. Another search found more signs of Europeans—the ruins of a brick building, a large heap of coal, wood chips from the ship's timbers—and a human skull.

The next year, Samuel Hearne led a search party to the cove on Marble Island. They found many graves. The hulks of two ships lay in five fathoms of water. There was a dwelling, as well as various relics that belonged to Knight's ships.

A year later, Hearne returned to interview the old Inuit who had visited the island when some of Knight's party were alive. Only then did he learn details of the crew's horrible fate. The Inuit told him that in the late fall of 1719, after the wrecking of Knight's ships, about 50 men had built a house. Many died during that first winter. By the end of the second winter, only 20 men survived. The following summer there were 5 men left alive. Most poignant of all is the Inuit accounting of the demise of the last 2 men to survive on the island. The Inuit told Hearne that the men frequently went to the top of a rock and intensely searched to the south and east, looking for a rescue vessel. Then one died. The other started digging a grave to bury his friend and died in the attempt.

During their lonely ordeal, trading vessels from York Factory were sailing along that coast, perhaps two-days' sailing time from the island. No one had told them that Knight's expedition was missing. No one seemed to care.

The mystery surrounding the Knight expedition on Marble Island continues to this day. Why did Knight go there? Was he too proud to seek shelter at an HBC post? Why did he decide to brave the severe winter on Marble Island without winter clothing? Did a storm drive the ships into the cove for safety and then seal them in with ice? What really happened?

Marble Island is a barren, treeless and desolate rock, 483 kilometres from the Churchill River and 25 kilometres from the mainland. There are no animals for fresh meat. In 1885, Charles Tuttle wrote of Marble Island that "the winds of almost perpetual winter blow in pitiless and withering blasts."

According to Inuit legend, Marble Island was transformed from an iceberg by the spirits as they answered the plea of an old woman on the iceberg to let her die on land. Out of respect for the Inuit legend, first-time visitors must not walk on the land. They must crawl ashore to avoid offending the spirits of the dead who dwell at Marble Island.

Henry Kelsey

Henry Kelsey was barely 17 years old in 1687 when he was sent on his first wilderness journey for the Hudson's Bay Company. He delivered letters from York Factory to Fort Severn—a 320-kilometre trek.

Kelsey had done such a admirable job that the HBC corporate office instructed that "the Boy Henry Kelsey be sent to Churchill River with Thomas Savage, because we are informed that he is a very active Lad . . . " The following summer, young Kelsey and a Native boy were transferred to the edge of the Barren Lands, north of Churchill River. The shore still had ice. Their task was to "bring a commerce to Northern Indians." The two young men began to worry about the success of their mission after not seeing any Native peoples, despite 320 kilometres of searching. At that time of year, the mosquitoes were ravenous, and there was no place to hide. Although the harsh subarctic environment was inhospitable, it did provide a unique opportunity for Kelsey. On July 9, 1689, he was the first European known to have seen a musk ox.

It was a difficult journey. On July 2, Kelsey wrote, "At noon it rained hard having no shelter but ye heavens for a Cannope nor no wood to make a fire." And it was danger- ous. After a six-week journey, he had to shoot three treach- erous waterfalls on a raft in order to reach his ship's pick-up point on the Churchill River.

This trip was a reconnaissance for the two-year mission he would tackle the following year. The HBC wanted to show their shareholders that efforts were being made to travel inland for trade. Kelsey was selected to make this long trek to travel west, deeper into Native country than anyone else had before him. His mission was not a simple voyage of exploration. His task was to meet with Native groups and invite them to come and trade with the Hudson's Bay Company. He carried tobacco from Brazil, as well as glass beads, hatchets and kettles.

Kelsey was a good choice. He spoke the Cree language, was familiar with Native methods of travel and knew the customs of the country. But his poetic travel records reveal his apprehension about the trip.

> In sixteen hundred & ninety-th year
> I set forth as plainly may appear
> And for my masters interest I did soon
> Sett from ye house (York Fort) ye twelth of June
> Then up ye River I with heavy heart
> Did take my way and from all English part
> To live amongst ye Natives of this place
> If god permits me for one two years space
> The Inland Country of Good report hath been
> By Indians but by English not yet seen.

Travelling with a Cree companion, he headed southwest from York Factory to the sheltered bend in the Saskatchewan River, just below what is today The Pas, Manitoba. They wintered with the northern Cree, then followed the

Assiniboine River southwest across the Saskatchewan River and the Red River, onto the great plains of western Canada, perhaps as far as Touchwood Hills, Saskatchewan. While in this area, Kelsey was the first man of European origin to see the huge herds of thousands and thousands of free-roaming buffalo (bison).

This two-year journey was also difficult and dangerous. Not only was the terrain unfamiliar, but he was travelling among tribes who were often at war with each other. He tried to mediate and promote peace among the Native peoples, even attempting to make trade treaties. He went buffalo hunting with the Native peoples and kept a day-to-day journal under difficult conditions, writing all his entries in rhyme.

> Because I was alone & no friend could find
> And once yet in my travels I was left behind
> Which struck fear and terror into me
> But still I was resolved this same Country for to see.

Kelsey was the first HBC man to undertake an inland voyage. It seems he was accompanied by a Cree woman for much of it. As later explorers discovered, an inland journey by non-Aboriginals was doomed to failure if they were not accompanied by a Native woman. The famous Chipewyan guide, Matonabbee (who led Samuel Hearne's successful 1771–72 expedition) told Hearne that his first two expeditions had failed primarily because there were no women accompanying him. The HBC explorer Anthony Henday admits it was the Cree woman, his "bedfellow," who provided invaluable service on his epic inland journey in the 1750s.

Kelsey knew his success depended on having a Native woman by his side. When he returned to York Factory in 1692, he was accompanied by a Cree "wife" and insisted she be allowed to enter York Factory. History doesn't record what happened to her, although we do know that Henry later returned to England and to his English wife, Elizabeth.

Unfortunately, Kelsey's reports from his amazing expedition were received and forgotten. The HBC failed to use any of his findings, nor place his wanderings on a map. Today, Kelsey's journals from 1690 to 1692 have become a classic travelogue of early North America. They are the first account of the life and customs of Native peoples on the prairies. Later, Kelsey was the first to record the Inuit and other Native languages. He spent long winter nights working on a Native dictionary, which was published in 1710.

Kelsey was a dominant figure in the HBC's early years. He was present at York Factory during the stormy years when it was captured twice by the French and during the great 1697 sea battle in Hudson Bay. He subsequently officiated at the surrender of York Factory. He was deputy to Governor Knight when the remarkable Chipewyan woman Thanadelthur was at York Factory. In 1719, the year Knight disappeared, Kelsey commanded an expedition to explore the northwest coast of Hudson Bay. Two Inuit boys accompanied him so he could learn their language. And during the years 1718 to 1722, he was governor of all the Company's forts in the region.

Kelsey's career with the HBC spanned 59 years. He was the first apprentice who rose up through the ranks to become one of the HBC's senior overseas governors. Yet, when he died in 1730, his wife and children in England were left in poverty.

Mrs. Sergeant and Mrs. Maurice

In April 1683, Henry Sergeant was appointed governor and chief commander of all the trading posts in Hudson Bay. The London Committee liked him and considered him well-qualified for the job.

When he sailed for the Hudson Bay, Sergeant brought along his wife, his young son and probably one daughter. Also accompanying him were his wife's companion and maid, Mrs. Maurice, his chaplain Reverend John French and three male servants. Documents refer to his "parcell of women," but they deserve much more respect and historical recognition. Mrs. Sergeant and Mrs. Maurice were the first English women to live by the bay.

Their first winter was spent at Moose Factory. The following year (1684), the family moved their household to the newly constructed HBC post at Fort Albany, on the south side of the river. Little is known about these women pioneers—not even their first names. No journals or notes have been found recording their feelings about the three years they spent on the Hudson Bay, but they did live through an incredible period of HBC history. Their survival is a testament to their bravery.

When the HBC supply ship arrived at the bay in 1685, there was a message for Mrs. Maurice to return home to England. Her father was ill and needed her. She packed, said goodbye to Mrs. Sergeant and in December boarded the *Success*, the HBC ship heading back to England. It was very late for any ship to navigate through the dangerous Hudson Strait. And luck wasn't on the ship's side. Despite its name, the *Success* was wrecked on the northwest coast of the bay. Mrs. Maurice survived the shipwreck and spent the winter of 1685–86 at Charles Fort, waiting for the next summer's supply ship.

On the fateful night of July 15, 1686, Mrs. Sergeant was without her companion, Mrs. Maurice. Up to that point, life at Fort Albany was, for Mrs. Sergeant, somewhat lonely and a bit boring, but certainly safe and predictable. All that was about to change. That evening, just before eight o'clock, Mrs. Sergeant and her husband, Henry, were sitting down for supper with their children.

Dining was among the high points of Mrs. Sergeant's daily life in the isolated wilderness of the bay. Because her husband was governor, life was much better for her than for the others stationed at the fort. Henry had three manservants to assist and serve him. His wife had only Mrs. Maurice. However, on this night, all the residents of the fort, no matter what their social status, were greatly rattled and shaken.

The manservant was pouring dinner wine in the Sergeants' glasses. Suddenly, out of the silent night—KABOOM!—a cannon shot fired through the house, passing under the servant's arm. Before anyone could react, another cannon shot flew in front of Mrs. Sergeant's face. She fainted. The French commandos had arrived. Fort Albany was under attack.

The fort was under siege for two days. Henry Sergeant's main concern was the safety of his wife and children. Some reports say that he had told his men that if the French were to breach the fort, every man must take care of himself, and that he would take care of himself and his family. Years later, when interviewed in England by Daniel Defoe (a chronicler of English life and the author of *Robinson Crusoe*), Sergeant confessed that they were not prepared to withstand an attack by European troops and that they had no choice but to surrender.

Two days after the traumatic attack, the family chaplain, Reverend French, courageously ventured out with a makeshift white flag to end the siege. He made arrangements for the wine-on-the-river surrender meeting between Henry Sergeant and the French commander, de Troyes. After the surrender, Mrs. Sergeant was shipped with the other English prisoners to Charlton Island to wait for the arrival of a ship that would take them to England. Much to her surprise, her companion on the prisoner ship was none other than her maid, Mrs. Maurice. Of course, Mrs. Sergeant had thought her maid was safely away in England with her father.

Mrs. Maurice had been taken prisoner by the French at Charles Fort earlier that June, where she was wintering after being shipwrecked on the *Success*. She had been wounded in the attack on Charles Fort and transferred to Fort Albany by the French, where she rejoined Mrs. Sergeant.

After the commando raids, the French waited for the annual HBC supply ship, *Happy Return*, to arrive in the bay. Their plan was to seize its cargo, put their English prisoners on board and let it sail back to England. Until its arrival the French were forced to provide provisions for the prisoners on Charlton Island. It was July and they expected their English prisoners to be gone before winter. They all waited eagerly, both English and French, for the supply ship to arrive. They waited and waited. But the *Happy Return* had become lodged in the ice in July and never made it to Charlton Island.

With over 90 people on the island, supplies were running low. The French commander, d'Iberville, was desperate to get rid of his 52 prisoners before winter. He decided to release them to the two HBC posts still under English control. These posts were York Factory (also called York, Hayes Fort and York Fort) on the Nelson River and the Severn River Fort (sometimes called Fort Churchill or New Severn).

Sergeant and 30 prisoners (including Mrs. Sergeant, their children and Mrs. Maurice) were forced aboard the *Colleton*,

a wrecked HBC ship that the French had refloated and repaired. With scanty provisions, they set out on a dangerous
voyage hoping to reach York Factory. The other 21 prisoners,
all men, were abandoned on Charlton Island. They eventually followed d'Iberville to Moose Factory, where they were
not welcomed by the French. Some of the men went to live
with Native peoples for the winter, while the others survived
by begging outside the fort. The following year, they left by
canoe for the St. Lawrence. They had the distinction of being
the first Englishmen to travel overland from the Hudson Bay.

At York Factory, Mrs. Sergeant and Mrs. Maurice endured a terrible winter. The fort was already overcrowded, a
situation made worse with the arrival of the surviving crew
of the *Happy Return*, whose non-arrival at Charlton Island
earlier that summer had caused the whole crisis.

Unbeknownst to Henry Sergeant, the *Happy Return*
had carried an order for him to immediately hand over his
command. However, the order was lost in the shipwreck.
So, Henry, still thinking he was the governor and chief
commander, used his power to ensure his family was well
treated at the fort. Mrs. Sergeant and Mrs. Maurice were
used to a certain standard of treatment. Even though starvation was all around them, Henry made sure they received
adequate provisions.

During that dreadful winter at York Factory, 20 of the
30 survivors from the Fort Albany raid died. The London
Committee soberly reported that 20 of their men had died,

"frozen and Starved, and some faine to be Eaten up by the rest of the Company."

Mrs. Sergeant and Mrs. Maurice lived through harrowing times. Shipwreck. Commando attacks. Battles. Death and destruction. Imprisonment. Dangerous voyages. Hostile environments. Starvation. Cannibalism. And then a ten-week homeward voyage on the *Colleton* across the unpredictable waters of the Atlantic Ocean.

No other non-Aboriginal woman would step foot on any HBC post for the next 119 years—by order of the Company —until Isabel Gunn surreptitiously arrived in 1806.

Isabel Gunn

Twenty-six-year-old Isabel Gunn of Orkney put on male clothing, headed for the docks and boarded the *Prince of Wales*, an HBC supply ship headed for Rupert's Land with Henry Hanwell as captain. Isabel went as a man (calling herself John Fubbister) because European women were not allowed at fur-trading posts. She had just signed a three-year contract to work for the Hudson's Bay Company as a labourer. Isabel knew that for the next three years she would have to pretend to be a man, working in an isolated, harsh land she had never seen. Why did she go? She went because the man she loved was somewhere in Rupert's Land, employed by the HBC. And she wanted to join him.

On July 29, 1806, Captain Henry Hanwell slipped out of Stromness Harbour and out into the Atlantic Ocean. The voyage was an ordeal—the unpredictable stormy waters of the Atlantic Ocean, the fog and the ice floes of the Hudson Strait and the terrifying sounds of grinding, crunching ice. One out of every three HBC ships sailing the route were lost at sea.

The *Prince of Wales* arrived at Moose Factory in the third week in August. Throughout the voyage, Isabel had been vigilant about remembering who she was: John Fubbister, HBC labourer. From here, the Orkney men were transported to various northern posts on the Hudson Bay. On August 27, Isabel boarded an HBC shallop and headed for Fort Albany.

Two weeks after arriving at Albany, she was assigned to a brigade to take supplies and trading goods to Henley House. The party included fellow Orkney men John Scarth and James Brown. They travelled through rapids and fast-moving waters, loaded and unloaded cargo and then headed back to Albany. It was a gruelling 19-day journey.

The months wore on and no one suspected that John Fubbister was really Isabel Gunn, an Orkney woman. Even the man who shared her log hut, John Scarth, did not know that she was a woman. Often when Scarth returned from hunting he would find her sitting by the fire crying. Scarth noticed that Fubbister did very little work and always seemed to be sad, but thought the lad was homesick.

As the months wore on, Isabel must have worried that she would be found out and shipped back to Orkney without finding her lost love. One night, her ruse was discovered. In an interview, Donald Murray, a friend of John Scarth's, recalled the night Isabel's hut-mate found out she was not a man. "One night, Scart [Scarth] had been at the master's house until late at night, and on his return to the cabin discovered the true sex of his partner. He at once told the frightened woman that he would go to Mr. Goodwin [the man in charge of the HBC posts on the Assiniboine River] with the news, but she fell on her knees and begged him not to reveal her identity."

Scarth, almost 20 years her senior, agreed to keep the secret. They continued to live together in the log hut as before, but it wasn't long before the two became intimate, and Isabel became pregnant some time in the spring.

Life at the HBC posts became extremely busy in springtime. On May 21, both Isabel and Scarth were part of a brigade of three large boats and three *bateaux* taking the inland cargo up the river to Martens Falls. They returned on June 19, with a cargo of furs and castoreum. Three days later, Isabel left again to take cargo to Marten Falls, but this time she didn't come back. She was being sent to Pembina to cook for Donald (Mad) MacKay.

It was a long route to Pembina. After passing Osnaburgh House and Lac Seul, they paddled the Winnipeg River and up the Red River. It was in Pembina that Isabel realized she was carrying a child. During the last week of December, Isabel and other HBC workers trekked across the frozen

Pembina River to take Christmas greetings to Alexander Henry's trading post. Henry looked after the interests of the rival North West Company. The two posts were across from each other at the mouth of the Pembina River.

When the others returned to the HBC post on December 29, 1807, Isabel, still posing as a man, asked Alexander Henry if she could remain at his house for a bit longer as the walk back across the river might be too dangerous. Isabel knew she was close to giving birth. Henry wrote in his journal, "I was surprised at the fellow's demand, however, I told him to sit down and warm himself. I returned to my own room, where I had not been long before he sent one of my people, requesting the favour of speaking with me. Accordingly I stepped down to him, and was much surprised to find him extended on the hearth, uttering dreadful lamentations; he stretched out his hands towards me, and in piteous tones begged to me be kind to a poor, helpless, abandoned wretch, who was not of the sex I had supposed, but an unfortunate Orkney girl, pregnant, and actually in childbirth. In saying this she opened her jacket, and displayed a pair of beautiful, round, white breasts; she further informed me of the circumstances that had brought her into this state . . . In about an hour she was safely delivered of a fine boy, and that same day she was conveyed home in my *cariole*, where she soon recovered."

Isabel stayed at Pembina with her newborn son, James Scarth, until spring. On May 28, 1808, she left for Fort

83

Albany with Hugh Heney's party. The relationship between Isabel and Scarth became the talk of the HBC, however, only brief mention appears in the Company's journals. One reference was from Thomas Vincent, acting chief of Fort Albany. After meeting the returning party at Marten Falls he wrote, "One of Mr. Heney's 'men', was found to be a woman debauched (so she says) by John Scarth, by whom she has a Child." A more detailed reference was made by Donald Murray, John Scarth's friend and an original 1815 Selkirk settler in the Red River. "I remember perfectly well the case of the Orkney girl you have written about, who is mentioned, you tell me, in Alexander Henry's journal. Of course, I was not in this country in 1807 when the affair occurred, but I knew well the man (Scarth) who was connected with it, and the story was common talk for many a year after we arrived in this country . . . It was when there [Pembina] that she made a discovery as to her condition and went over to Mr. Henry at the Northwest fort, and was delivered of a child to the great surprise of all the people in the country, who had never suspected that she was a woman."

Once back at Fort Albany, Isabel was relegated to being a washerwoman, a role she neither liked nor did well. But she did not want to go back to Orkney. The Fort Albany schoolmaster, William Harper, wrote on September 5, 1808, "The Governor intends to make her a nurse for the Scholars, as she seems not inclined to go home . . . "

Isabel and her son stayed for another year at Fort Albany.

Then on September 14, 1809, the HBC discharged her from service. Six days later, she and her son James boarded the HBC ship, the *Prince of Wales*, and headed back to Orkney. The father of her child, John Scarth, always acknowledged that James was his child, and Isabel the mother. He visited Orkney in 1812, returned to HBC service at York Factory and then retired to the Red River Colony in 1818. He married a widow, Nelly Saunderson, in 1822.

Isabel's legacy is an incredible story of determination, challenge, strength and courage. She was a romantic and an adventurer and thus well suited for the fur trade, despite her gender.

Thanadelthur

In the spring of 1713, there was a brutal attack by the Cree on a group of Chipewyan. Most of the Chipewyan were killed, but a remarkable woman named Thanadelthur (meaning "marten shake") and two others were captured and became Cree prisoners.

It wasn't until the fall of 1714, while camped on the north shore of the Nelson River, that they managed to escape. Thanadelthur and another woman started travelling to the Barren Lands to find their people. The Chipewyan were nomadic people with their homeland spread across northern Saskatchewan and up into the Northwest Territories. Their traditional enemy, the Cree, lived to their south and east.

About the same time that Thanadelthur escaped from

the Cree, Governor James Knight arrived at York Factory from England to begin his term as governor-in-chief of the bay. The paths of Thanadelthur and James Knight soon crossed. Knight arrived to officially take back all of the HBC fur-trading posts from the French, posts given back to the HBC under the terms of the 1713 Treaty of Utrecht.

As Knight was settling in at York Factory, Thanadelthur and her friend were desperately struggling to stay alive. The wilderness trekking was very difficult and they were cold and hungry. Realizing they would not make it home by winter, they turned back and headed for York Factory.

Thanadelthur's companion died along the way. Five days later, Thanadelthur came across the tracks of a goose-hunting party of HBC men. She followed them to their tents at Ten Shilling Creek, slightly upstream from York Factory. Starving and exhausted, she stumbled into the camp.

On November 24, 1714, one of the goose-hunters took Thanadelthur to York Factory. Earlier that month, another Chipewyan woman had also sought refuge at the fort, saying she had been a prisoner of the Cree. Knight had called her Slave Woman and talked to her several times about her people (the Slave were a tribe of the Chipewyan). He noted in his journals that she had valuable information about establishing trade with her people, the Chipewyan. He was convinced such trade would bring huge profits.

But Slave Woman died on November 22, 1714, and Knight lamented the lost opportunity to gain more information.

Two days later, Thanadelthur arrived. Knight was thrilled to have another Slave Woman at the post. He continued with his plan of promoting peace between the different Native groups in the area because with peaceful times the local people could concentrate on processing furs rather than making war. Knight listened carefully when Thanadelthur explained that her people would not come to the bay to trade with the HBC because the Cree had guns and they were afraid to cross Cree territory. She told Knight she wanted to help him bring peace to her people.

In the spring of 1715, Knight organized a peace mission to the Chipewyan, led by the HBC's William Stuart and guided by Thanadelthur. A contingent of 150 Home Cree also accompanied them. (Home Cree were the Cree who lived around the fort and provided the HBC with fresh game and fish.) They left on June 27, 1715, headed for the Barren Lands. Their mission was to negotiate a peace between the Cree and the Chipewyan. Thanadelthur was instructed to tell her people that the English would build a fort at the foot of the Churchill River in the fall. Knight, who had an obsession with gold, instructed Stuart to look for minerals, particularly gold, while on the mission.

Knight gave specific instructions to Stuart about Thanadelthur. He was, above all, to protect Slave Woman. Their mission was a harrowing venture. Sickness and starvation forced most of the Cree to abandon the group. Only Stuart, Thanadelthur, the Cree captain and about a dozen of his followers were left when they chanced upon a gruesome discovery. Sprawled in the bloody snow were the bodies of nine Chipewyan slaughtered by the Cree at the edge of the tree line. Fearing revenge, the group's remaining Cree wanted to turn back immediately, but Thanadelthur convinced them to wait 10 days. During that time, she would travel—alone— to find her people and return with them to make peace.

Thanadelthur followed the tracks of the Chipewyan who had escaped the massacre. It took only a few days for her to find them. Convincing them to return with her into Cree territory was not an easy task. Intense debate went on for hours. Then days. Thanadelthur, a passionate orator, talked so fervently that her voice became hoarse. She was determined to convince the Chipewyan to make peace with the Cree. She wanted her people to trade with the English and to be able to trade without fear.

Stuart and the Cree waited anxiously for Thanadelthur. Would she survive alone in the woods? They were losing hope that she would return. Then, finally, on the tenth day Thanadelthur dramatically reappeared at the camp. Two Chipewyan emissaries stood by her side, but no other Chipewyan were in sight. It wasn't until Stuart came out to meet them that she signalled to the rest of the delegation that it was safe to approach. Over 150 Chipewyan streamed to the camp from their hiding places in the forest.

The peace talks began. First, Thanadelthur and the Cree captain assured the Chipewyan that the Cree party bore no responsibility for the Chipewyan massacre. It was time to negotiate peace. Stuart knew that Native people were great speechmakers, but he was amazed at Thanadelthur's powerful use of words. Some of her speeches were long, full of emotion, wit, sarcasm and irony. Other times, her words were softer and somewhat poetic. But always she was eloquent and persuasive.

Finally, after much negotiation, Thanadelthur successfully negotiated a peace between the warring tribes. Knight wrote in his notes, " Wm. Stuart tells me he never seen any of such spirit in his life. Indeed she has a Devilish spirit . . . "

The successful expedition arrived back at York Factory in May 1716, accompanied by the Cree and a small group of Chipewyan. During the winter, Thanadelthur married a Chipewyan by the name of Lothario and learned to speak English. She continued to tell Knight alluring stories of her country's rich minerals, broad rivers, straits with great tides, and of a tribe of white-bearded giants (perhaps the legendary blond Inuit of Victoria Island).

Thanadelthur understood how valuable her interpreting and guiding skills were to Knight and the HBC. She thoroughly enjoyed, and exploited, the influence she had on him. Enthusiastically, she planned her mission to the Barren Lands for the following summer. But fate had other plans for her.

On January 11, 1717, Knight records that Slave Woman had become very ill and that he was expecting her death at any time. When she was close to death, she called the HBC's clerk Robert Norton (who would have been her partner on the next expedition) to her bedside. She told him not to be afraid of her people and that her brother and her people would love him and not let him want for anything.

Thanadelthur died on February 5, 1717, and was buried at York Factory. Her life had been short—barely 25 years—but she left her mark as a diplomat for her people and helped open the northern fur trade. Knight later wrote, "She was one of a very high spirit and of the firmest resolution that ... ever I see any Body in my Days and of great courage and forecast, also endowed with an extraordinary vivacity..."

7

The Rivalry Continues

DURING ITS FIRST 100 YEARS of operation, the Hudson's Bay Company had successfully operated with only seven trading posts, all strategically located at the mouths of rivers flowing into the Hudson and James bays. Native peoples annually travelled long distances by birchbark canoe and overland to transport their harvest of furs to the HBC posts. All the HBC men had to do was wait and be prepared to trade. Except for the inland expeditions made by Henry Kelsey from 1690 to 1692 and Anthony Henday in 1754, there had been no initiatives to expand into the interior.

The HBC's rivalry with the French *coureurs de bois* ended when Britain defeated New France in 1763. But a new, more dangerous trading rival was emerging from the vacuum left by the Montreal fur traders—one that would bring the HBC into a deadly war and to the brink of destruction.

It was around this time that the HBC took notice that its fur-trade profits were beginning to erode. First Nations trading groups heading toward the HBC forts on the bay were being intercepted en route by competing fur traders. Business was falling as fewer fur-laden canoes made it to the HBC posts. In 1773, York Factory had only 8,000 "made beaver," compared with an annual average of 30,000 in the ten-year period from 1756 to 1766. A made beaver was the standard of trade in the fur trade, equalling one good-quality adult beaver pelt.

The Hudson's Bay Company finally realized it had to establish inland trading posts to be competitive. And in 1774 the London Committee sent Samuel Hearne to establish Cumberland House, its first permanent inland post. Hearne set off in the spring of 1774 and selected a site on the Saskatchewan River called Pine Island Lake (now Cumberland Lake in Saskatchewan) at the junction of several water routes. The site was about 95 kilometres west of modern-day The Pas, in northwestern Manitoba.

After clearing the ground, Hearne and his men built a low-slung log bunker with a plank roof, using moss for caulking and insulation. It was a primitive building, but it served as the first inland post for HBC. The men stored their supplies in a warehouse at the east end of their shelter. Hearne, an experienced expedition leader, knew the winter

Detail from oil painting entitled *The Pioneers' Highway*

would be difficult. It was the first time he was faced with men not accustomed to wilderness. Though they were stocked with trading goods and supplies, the HBC men almost starved the first winter, as they had brought along very little extra food. An added element of concern was the 150 rival traders set up in the area around the fort. But Hearne kept relations with the other traders cordial and no confrontations occurred.

The new HBC post was successful. At spring breakup, Hearne led a flotilla of 32 canoes laden with 1,647 made beaver to York Factory. In their third season, Cumberland House increased its trade to 6,162 made beaver.

For the next 50 years, the HBC traders would criss-cross the vast Rupert's Land, from the Great Lakes to the Pacific, rapidly establishing trading posts. Between 1774 and 1821, the HBC opened 242 new inland posts, although some of these were short-lived. And, for the first time in its history, the HBC encouraged colonization on its land.

The Emergence of the North West Company

By the 1700s, the Hudson's Bay Company was routinely re-cruiting Orkney men to work on the bay. By 1799, over three-quarters of the HBC men were from Orkney. The Orkney men brought practical skills that the HBC needed—basic literacy, fishing knowledge and boat construction. The men were an integral part of the HBC operations, although few rose to the powerful higher ranks.

When Britain defeated New France at the Plains of Abraham in 1759, a new group of entrepreneurs emerged as fierce fur-trading competitors to the HBC. They were young men from mainland Scotland, who joined with the former *coureurs du bois* and a few Irish and American fur traders to take over the control of the Montreal fur trade. The HBC men called them peddlars.

In 1784, the "peddlars" from Montreal launched the North West Company (the company and its men were known also as the Nor'westers), a partnership of nine different fur-trading groups, including the powerful Montreal Coalition. They pushed deeper into the interior of Canada, challenging the HBC for control of the fur trade. They openly defied the Royal Charter, often building their forts right beside those of the HBC. They were energetic men, sometimes violent, who quickly built a competing fur-trading empire that stretched to the Pacific Ocean.

Tensions were rising in the intense fur-trade rivalry between the Hudson's Bay Company and the North West Company. Both sides were becoming more brazen and more physical in their attempts to eliminate their competition.

One confrontation occurred in September 1809, when a Nor'wester clerk, Aeneas Macdonnell, and his men seized HBC goods from a Native trader at Eagle Lake, northeast of Lake of the Woods. When the HBC men rushed to save the Company's property, Macdonnell slashed HBC servant John Mowat. The wounded Mowat grabbed a pistol and shot and killed Macdonnell. Both Mowat and another HBC servant, James Tate, were arrested by the Nor'westers and sent to Rainy Lake. Mowat spent the winter in chains. In May, the two wounded men were sent to Fort William, the Nor'westers depot on Lake Superior, with Tate forced to paddle. At Fort William, Mowat was kept in chains 14 hours a day. His body became covered with festering boils and cuts, but he was not allowed to have medicine. In mid-August, a sobbing Mowat was sent by canoe, bound in chains, on a five-week voyage to Montreal for trial. He was found guilty and sentenced to six months in jail and branded on his left thumb. When he was finally released, a deranged and branded Mowat vanished in northern New York.

The violent incidents kept increasing. There were ambushes and kidnappings as traders hunted traders. Forts were seized and wives and children terrorized. But the catalyst for pushing the two enemies to an all-out war was the attempt by Lord Selkirk to establish the Red River settlement in Rupert's Land.

The Red River Colony

The Hudson's Bay Company controlled the land, the people and the resources in an enormous area. First Nations people lived on the land, but there were no plans for European colonies or settlements until Lord Selkirk (Thomas Douglas, the Fifth Earl of Selkirk) decided to purchase a grant of land in Rupert's Land from the HBC to give to poor Scottish farmers. He had carried out other colonization projects. In 1803, he had successfully settled 800 Highlanders in Prince Edward Island. A similar attempt in 1804 at Baldoon, near Lake St. Clair, had failed.

Lord Selkirk's project to establish settlements was inspired by a book published by Nor'wester explorer Alexander Mackenzie, *Voyage from Montreal on the River St. Lawrence to the Frozen and Pacific Ocean, in the years 1789 and 1793*. Selkirk wanted to help poor Scottish farmers find land to farm. North America had land to spare. In order to carry out his plan, Selkirk secured enough stock that he gained control of the Hudson's Bay Company. He then secured a grant from the HBC for a huge tract of land in the Red River area and beyond. The land covered 300,000 square kilometres in what is now Manitoba, North Dakota, Minnesota and Saskatchewan. The grant also gave authority for control over the lives of all residents living in the area ... Europeans, Métis and First Nations.

The Métis

But the granted land already was homeland to a new nation of people—the Métis. They were the offspring of relationships between First Nation "country wives" and (primarily) Scottish and French fathers who had worked in the fur trade. While some of the men took their Native wives and children with them when they left and settled elsewhere, most did not.

The Métis lived in the Red River area, providing the Nor'westers with pemmican (the food staple of the First Nations). The North West Company bought the pemmican from the Métis for their voyageurs and trading posts. Without pemmican, many Nor'westers might have starved to death. Pemmican provided maximum nourishment with minimum bulk and weight. Women prepared pemmican by cutting the buffalo meat into thin strips and drying it in the sun. It was then pounded into a powder on a buffalo hide, mixed in equal quantity with buffalo grease and flavoured with berries (cranberries, saskatoons, blueberries). The pemmican was then sewn into 42-kilogram bags of buffalo hide (42 kilograms is the weight that voyageurs traditionally carried per load over portages). Pemmican was the perfect food for the peddlars and voyageurs to carry. It could be eaten raw, broiled over a campfire or used as the main ingredient for stew or chowder.

Neither the Métis nor the North West Company welcomed British settlement in the Red River region. The Nor'westers considered the Red River area their land. The proposed settlement would run alongside the Nor'wester's main water-routes to the Athabasca River. The North West Company saw the colonization as a plan by the HBC to drive them out of the area. And the Métis felt threatened because they feared the settlers would compete for the buffalo, their main source of food and livelihood.

The Settlers Arrive

Back in London, three North West Company men who were also shareholders in HBC, Alexander Mackay, Edward Ellice and Simon McGillivray, tried to stop Selkirk's plan for settlement. Ellice warned Selkirk that the Nor'westers might destroy the colony. Ellice considered his Nor'wester wintering partners as "a set of men utterly destitute of all moral principle or the feelings of honour prevalent in civilized society, men who were in general of the lowest origin, selected from among the indigent relatives of the leading partners." He added, ominously, "They would not scruple to commit any crime which was necessary to effect the views of their associates in the concern."

But Selkirk didn't listen. Selkirk's first group of settlers arrived at Hudson Bay in 1811, just before freeze-up. Their first winter in the New World was terrible. They were forced to go to York Factory where they were to winter. But when they got there, they were sent on to Port Nelson. The settlers had no shelter or provisions and many died of starvation, exposure and scurvy. In the spring, only 22 of the original 105 travelled down from Hudson Bay to the Red River area. There they built a fort called Fort Douglas.

Another group arrived in October. When they arrived in the settlement area, there was no shelter ready for them (even for a woman, Mrs. McLean, who had given birth on the way). The first group had only arrived at the settlement a few months before. They were not capable of helping the new contingent of settlers as everyone was starving, both the first and the second wave of immigrants. The settlers avoided starvation that winter by buying pemmican from the North West Company. The following summer, the settlers tried farming but the crops were unsuccessful. Another winter passed, and there was little food. Death from starvation was a constant threat.

Tensions peaked dramatically when the colony's governor, Miles Macdonnell, made a proclamation on January 8, 1814, that made it illegal to take pemmican out of the colony. And later, Sheriff John Spencer seized 490 bags of pemmican from the North West Company.

This seizure raised the stakes, as the Nor'westers relied on pemmican for their long inland fur-trading trips. The North West Company worked out of Montreal and each spring their canoes left with goods and provisions for Fort William or for interior posts. Sometimes it would be a two or three month canoe trip to the north. As the Nor'westers could not use the Hudson Bay for transport, they had to transport their furs to Fort William and then on to Montreal.

Fort William was the North West Company's major inland trans-shipment point. Supplies and goods were shipped there for distribution inland. Winter produce (furs) from the wintering posts was sent to Fort William, then to England via Montreal. Fort William was also the headquarters for the Nor'westers annual business meetings between the wintering partners (also called proprietors) and the Montreal agents. The wintering partners would decide what they wanted in their annual "outfits" and the Montreal agents would transport the goods, provisions and supplies to Fort William by canoe and schooner. The Montreal agents were the wholesalers and the wintering partners the retailers.

The North West Company could not stand by and have their pemmican supply routes disrupted or their pemmican seized. They decided to destroy the Red River Colony by removing its leaders and dispersing the settlers. The Nor'wester Duncan Cameron, pretending to be a military officer, ordered the settlers to evacuate the colony, promising them a better life in Upper Canada. Of the 200 settlers, 140 were to accompany him to Fort William, while the other 60 fled to Hudson Bay. Then Cameron completely destroyed the colony by setting it on fire.

After spending some time at Fort William, the Nor'westers loaded the colonists into heavy, open boats and forced them to row across the treacherous waters of Lake Superior and down Lake Huron to reach Upper Canada.

When the Red River Colony was re-established the following year (1815), the Nor'westers were convinced the HBC's goal was the total destruction of the North West Company. Tension continued to grow, until it reached a flashpoint at Seven Oaks, just outside of the HBC's Fort Douglas.

The Massacre at Seven Oaks

On June 18, 1816, freetrader Jean-Baptiste Lagimodière was returning to the Red River Colony after delivering a message to Selkirk in Montreal. The Nor'westers heard about his return expedition and sent Pierre Bonga and several Natives to stop him. They captured Lagimodière, beat him, arrested him and took him as prisoner to Fort William. This was one day before the massacre at Seven Oaks, where the Métis attacked and killed HBC governor Robert Semple and 20 settlers.

The Métis and their leader Cuthbert Grant positioned themselves at the group of trees known as Seven Oaks.

Governor Semple and his men came out of the fort heading towards the riverbank. François Boucher was sent by Grant to intercept them and ordered Semple and his group to lay down their arms. After a heated discussion, there was a scuffle, and as Semple attempted to seize Boucher's gun, Grant fired. Governor Semple was wounded. That one shot was the start of a six-year war between the two fur-trading rivals, the Hudson's Bay Company and the North West Company.

There was confusion and chaos. More shots were fired. Lieutenant Ener Holte, the Swedish veteran soldier who had come to settle in the Red River area, was the first to die. The Métis instantly slid down to the ground and used their horses to level their guns at Semple and his men. More settlers died. Return shots were fired. For a brief time, when the Métis were reloading their guns, the Semple survivors thought that the fighting was over—that they had won. They threw their hats in the air, but then gunfire once again surrounded them.

Grant had been trying to save Semple from being killed, but in the shooting frenzy a Métis named François Deschamps placed a gun to the governor's chest and shot him dead. An eyewitness survivor later wrote, "In a few minutes, almost all our people were killed or wounded."

In a matter of minutes, Governor Semple and his 20 men died at Seven Oaks. The settlement of Fort Douglas surrendered to Grant and the Métis.

After the attack, the North West Company distributed

gifts to the Métis as a reward for their service during the attack. They also took six settlers as prisoners, taking them back to Fort William. A few of them were bound in chains during the long canoe journey.

Selkirk was convinced, by the gifts given to the Métis, that the North West Company was directly involved in the murders. This launched a pamphlet war with both Selkirk and the North West Company publishing arguments about the purpose of the Métis gifts.

The Seizure of Fort William

The Battle of Seven Oaks took the rivalry to full-out deadly conflict. Hearing about the massacre, Selkirk headed to Fort William. He was leading a unit of British soldiers and 100 veteran Swiss, German and middle European mercenaries, who were providing their services in exchange for free land in the proximity of the Red River. On August 12, Selkirk's flotilla of canoes and boats made a spectacular entrance to the sound of drums, pipes and trumpets as they entered the Kaministiquia River and paddled past the fort. The people of Fort William watched in silence and waited.

Selkirk got right to work. He demanded and got the release of the Red River prisoners from the Nor'westers. He arrested the North West Company's chief executive officer and wintering partner, William McGillivray, for "conspiracy, treason, and being an accessory to murder." To avoid bloodshed, McGillivray surrendered peacefully. Then, 50 or 60 of Selkirk's soldiers, armed with pistols and swords, stormed the fort, capturing the other wintering partners.

The commander of the mercenary soldiers, Lieutenant Friederich von Graffenried, wrote about the attack. "Our men, however, were in no mood to fool around, and broke down the gate. Fortunately no shot was fired, otherwise we could not have restrained our men from plundering, and in all likelihood blood would have been spilled."

The soldiers secured the fort's papers for the night. But during the night, the partners gathered their papers by the armfuls and burned them in every fireplace available, including the great hall's fireplace and the kitchen stove. When Selkirk learned what had happened, he was furious and ordered a complete search of the fort. After finding hidden loaded guns and stashed gunpowder, he ordered the seizure of Fort William.

A few days later, Selkirk directed the canoes to get ready to transport the Nor'westers wintering partners to Upper Canada for trial. He assigned the Iroquois for the crews and sent the prisoner brigade out on Lake Superior on August 17. McGillivray warned Selkirk that one of the canoes was dangerously overloaded, putting lives at risk, but Selkirk refused to listen. Tragedy struck the brigade. On August 26, gale-force winds blew so hard that the overloaded canoe capsized in Lake Superior. Nine men drowned.

Selkirk occupied Fort William until spring and then left

for the Red River Colony. For the next six years, the violence continued between the two fur-trading competitors. Forts were destroyed and both sides took prisoners. Generally, the business became an armed battle rather than a trade in fur. When the courts of Upper Canada sorted out the various charges and counter-charges, there were 29 charges filed against HBC and Selkirk and 150 charges against the Nor'westers. Only one charge went through to conviction. Nor'wester Charles de Reinhard was sentenced to hang for murder.

The financial cost was high for both companies as they struggled to meet the rising legal costs amid declining revenue. The battles were ruining both companies.

8

A Historic Merger

BY THE EARLY NINETEENTH CENTURY, the North West Company was near collapse and the Hudson's Bay Company was stretched to its credit limit with the Bank of England. In 1820, the North West Company sent a delegation to London to negotiate a merger with the Hudson's Bay Company. At the time, the HBC had 76 posts and the North West Company had 97.

The two companies reached an agreement. The North West Company agents, Edward Ellice and Simon McGillivray, signed the merger on behalf of themselves, William McGillivray and the North West Company. It was a complex 12,000-word document, outlining a renewable contract effective for 21 years. William McGillivray, for whom Fort William was named, was weary, in poor health and on the verge of bankruptcy. In 1826, he died in England at age 49, leaving his daughters almost destitute.

The North West Company had been, for Ellice, only one of many business ventures, while for Simon McGillivray (who would later become penniless and move to Mexico) the company had provided access to London financial and social inner circles. Both had looked at the North West Company as a moneymaking venture. It was a business deal and they were only interested in the best dividend. Their focus on profit, rather than loyalty or sentimentality, echoed a similar line of thinking held by Radisson and des Groseilliers 150 years previous.

The HBC Wins Out

With the merger, the HBC had beaten its final rival. The area it controlled in North America grew to almost 7.8 million square kilometres. The HBC was granted a monopoly over the whole of British North America, except for the colonies already occupied on the Atlantic shore, the St. Lawrence and the lower Great Lakes. The HBC territory extended beyond Rupert's Land into Athabasca, across the Rocky and Coast mountains and into Oregon, and it ruled a trade empire from Labrador to the Pacific Ocean.

The Hudson's Bay Company had won on the battlefield and in the boardroom, and gained an unprecedented monopoly in the fur trade business.

The HBC trading post at Fort Edmonton, 1886

It was going to take an extraordinary person to effectively manage the huge new Hudson's Bay Company. The man selected was George Simpson, a short red-headed clerk in his thirties from London, England. He joined the HBC in 1820, and his first posting was Fort Wedderburn, the heartland of the violent fur-trading war. Five years later, in 1826, he was appointed the governor of all HBC operations in Rupert's Land. For the next 40 years, he dominated the company and aptly earned his nickname, The Little Emperor.

Simpson's goal was simple—to make money for the

HBC in the most cost-effective way. His first task was reorganizing the Company. He slashed the work force by 60 percent, closed trading posts and geared to a barebones operation. Everything had to operate with order and efficiency. He was an energetic man who led a fast pace. He moved across the continent by express canoe (with singing Iroquois voyageurs and his Highland piper), by horseback, by boat and by snowshoes—whatever it took to reach the far-flung posts of the HBC.

As the overseas governor, he ruled one of the largest empires on earth and did so successfully until his death in 1860. His legacy influenced the operations of the Hudson's Bay Company for many years.

After the Merger

The HBC made lucrative profits after the merger. It expanded its operations to link California, Russia, Hawaii and China. Anticipating a decrease in profits from the fur trade, it looked for new opportunities to successfully diversify, such as maritime shipping and selling wood to the Royal Navy.

The Hudson's Bay Company was open to explore any venture that would make money, including ice trading. When James Douglas was the HBC's chief factor on the Pacific coast in 1853 he signed a six-year lease with a group of San Francisco businessmen allowing their company, North West Ice Company, to cut glacial ice on all territory on coasts controlled by HBC. They paid the HBC a yearly rent of $14,000. The lease allowed the North West Ice Company to hire Native inhabitants of the area to cut and load the ice. But they were to be paid in goods purchased from the HBC, thus creating another source of profit for the Company.

During the first voyage, the group's ship, the barque (a sailing ship with three masts) *Fanny Major*, sailed into Frederick Sound (now Alaskan waters) and loaded up with 300 tons of compact blue ice. They hired a large number of Tlingit from the Stikine River as labourers. From reports by the ship's Captain Howard and chief trader John Kennedy, Douglas describes the incredible strength of the Tlingit, who worked in gruelling conditions. "About 500 Stikine Indians were mustered for that service, and they worked with an astonishing degree of ardour and tenacity of purpose, having in the first place cut a channel for the ship, through a space of two miles of solid ice, and carried the blocks of ice on their Shoulders from the iceberg about 1700 yards distant, to that point, the ground being at the time deeply covered with snow, and the labourers having neither shoes nor stockings to protect them from the cold."

The first shipment of ice sold quickly in San Francisco. Soon the group had five to seven ships loading glacial ice for new customers in Hong Kong and Hawaii. They built a large ice house in San Francisco and talked about another one in Honolulu. Then things started to go wrong. There was too much cargo melting on ocean voyages and there was fraud in the company. When it folded in 1856, the HBC considered entering the potentially lucrative ice business. They dropped the idea when another company secured the monopoly for the California ice trade.

Planning For Change

The key to the Hudson's Bay Company's success for over 300 years has been its willingness to change to meet new realities. When the trade in fur started to decline in the mid-1800s, the HBC turned to other commodities, such as selling coal and timber products to the Royal Navy and to other fleets. It operated its own side-wheeler, the S.S. *Beaver*, to sail to its posts in the north Pacific. The ship became a travelling fur post which, at many harbours, was surrounded by the canoes of Native traders eager to exchange their sea otter skins.

In 1860, almost 200 years after the Hudson's Bay Company had received its Royal Charter, the Company still ruled in the west. Business was good. The company's 286 shareholders were happy with their average annual dividend of 10 to 15 percent. There was peace in the fur trade.

But the Company knew that there were major changes coming to its empire. In 1857, British Parliament ended the royally chartered monopolies. The Red River Colonists, now ruled by HBC governors, wanted democracy and representative government. And in 1858, the Crown Colony of British Columbia was established.

Four years before the Confederation of Canada (1867), the HBC sent out word that it was ready to transfer its vast Rupert's Land to Canada. In 1870, it relinquished its rights of monopoly and sold its land holdings to the government of the Dominion of Canada. But the Hudson's Bay Company itself did not fade away. Today, it is still one of the world's oldest and most successful commercial empires.

Epilogue

THE HUDSON'S BAY COMPANY HAS had a long and fascinating history. Its past is aptly symbolized by its world-famous white wool blanket. The Hudson's Bay Company blankets were first introduced as a regular trade item over 200 years ago. A French trader, Monsieur Germain Maugenest, met with the London Committee in November 1779, presenting several suggestions to improve the company's growing inland trade. One of the suggestions was to add the "pointed blankets" as a regular trade item. After looking at some samples, the London Committee ordered 500 pairs of these blankets and shipped them for spring trading at the HBC posts. (All HBC blankets were originally sold as unseparated pairs that could be cut in the centre and separated at the time of sale.)

The "point" designation referred to the grading of each blanket according to weight and size. Points were identified by the indigo blue lines woven into each side of the blanket. A full point measured 14 centimetres, while a half point measured half of that length. The points ranged from 1 to 6, increasing by halves. Each point represented one made beaver pelt.

The first order was filled by Thomas Empson of Witney, Oxfordshire. Initially the blankets were woven on handlooms by master craftsmen. Later, they were mass-produced on machines. The wools were a blend of varieties from England, Wales, New Zealand and India, selected to create a water-resistant blanket which was strong, warm and soft.

Over time, the blanket has appeared in a variety of sizes and colours (ranging from light blue to indigo, green, scarlet, pastel, earth and jewel tones). Native peoples used the blankets as garments, for coats and robes. They particularly liked the 3-point blanket (with a wide coloured band across each end). When worn as a winter coat it provided the wearer with an impressive camouflage.

The Hudson's Bay Company blanket, a white wool blanket with distinctive bright bands of indigo, green, red and yellow, was introduced during the early 1800s and has endured to become an icon of Canada. This classic blanket—along with the Canadian beaver—are today's most recognized symbols of Canada and the historic fur trade.

Bibliography

Barnes, Michael. *Ride the Polar Bear Express*. Burnstown: The General Store Publishing House, 1996.

Binnema, Theodore, Gerhard J. Ens, and R.C. Macleod (editors). *From Rupert's Land to Canada*. Edmonton: University of Alberta Press, 2001.

Bryce, George. *The Remarkable History of the Hudson's Bay Company including That of the French Traders of North-western Canada and of the North-west, XY, and Astor Fur Companies*. Toronto: William Briggs, 1900.

Campbell, Marjorie Wilkins. *The North West Company* Vancouver: Douglas & McIntyre, 1983.

Fournier, Martin. *Pierre-Esprit Radisson, Merchant Adventurer 1637-1710*. Sillery: Les editions du Septentrion, 2002.

Innis, Harold A. *The Fur Trade in Canada: An Introduction to Canadian Economic History*. Toronto: University of Toronto Press, 1977.

McKay, Douglas. *The Honourable Company*. Toronto: McClelland and Stewart, 1966.

Morrison, Jean. *Superior Rendezvous-Place: Fort William in the Canadian Fur Trade*. Toronto: Natural Heritage Books, 2001.

Newman, Peter C. *Company of Adventurers*. Markham: Penguin Books Canada Limited, 1986.

Ray, Arthur J. *I Have Lived Here Since the World Began*. Toronto: Key Porter Books and Lester Publishing Limited, 1996.

Ray, Arthur J. *Indians in the Fur Trade: Their Role as Trappers, Hunters, and Middlemen in the Lands Southwest of Hudson Bay, 1660-1870*. Toronto: University of Toronto Press, 1974.

Tuttle, Charles R. *Our North Land: Being a Full Account of the Canadian North-West and Hudson's Bay Route, Together with a Narrative of the Experiences of the Hudson's Bay Expedition of 1884*. Toronto: C. Blackett Robinson, 1885.

Van Kirk, Sylvia. *Many Tender Ties, Women in Fur-Trade Society in Western Canada, 1670-1870*. Winnipeg: Watson & Dyer, 1980.

Willson, Beckles. *The Great Company: Being a History of the Honourable Company of Merchant-Adventurers Trading in Hudsons Bay*. Toronto: The Copp, Clark Company, Limited, 1899.

Index

Index

Acknowledgements

Writing a non-fiction book is somewhat like participating in a community project—there are so many people who contribute to make it happen. First of all, I would like to acknowledge and thank the many researchers, authors and writers who have previously published works about the Hudson's Bay Company. You have my respect and appreciation for your valuable contribution to the reference material on the history of the HBC and the fur trade in North America. A special thank you goes out to the staff at the HBC Archives for their invaluable assistance, and particularly to archival assistant Laurie Pottinger.

I'd also like to acknowledge the support of my children: Tania, who took time out of her vacation to review chapters, suggest changes and provide encouragement with her enthusiasm; Tami, who bolstered my confidence and constantly reassured me that I could finish writing the book by the deadline; and Cindi, who lifted my spirits with her unabashed pride that I was the world's greatest author. And a big thank you to my husband, Glenn, for his unconditional support of my work. He kept smiling as the piles of research material and the book's paperwork overflowed from my office to the living room and eventually covered most of the dining room table.

Special recognition goes to my book editor, Lesley Reynolds, for her positive suggestions and great editing, and to my publisher, Heritage House, for their professionalism and support of their authors.

About the Author

Elle Andra-Warner is an author, journalist and photographer based in Thunder Bay, Ontario. She specializes in writing about history, culture, travel, people and business and is the bestselling author of books about Canadian history, including *The Mounties: Tales of Adventure and Danger from the Early Days*, also published by Heritage House. Her award-winning articles appear regularly in major publications, and her regular newspaper columns on business, travel and history have been in print since 1994. As a corporate writer, her list of clients includes municipalities, corporations, travel associations and arts organizations.

A political studies graduate of Lakehead University, Elle is a member of the Professional Writers of Canada, Travel Media of Canada, the Writers Union of Canada and the Writers Guild of Alberta. She has given journalism workshops throughout Canada, is an online guest journalism lecturer for UCLA (University of California, Los Angeles), and is the co-editor of the Thunder Bay Historical Museum Society's annual journal, *Papers & Records*.

Estonian by heritage, Elle was born in a post–Second World War United Nations displaced persons camp for Estonians in Eckernforde, West Germany. She came to Canada with her parents, settling in Port Arthur, Ontario (now the city of Thunder Bay). Except for 2001–2004, when she lived in the Northwest Territories and Alberta, Thunder Bay has been Elle's home since her arrival in Canada.

More Great Books in the Amazing Stories Series

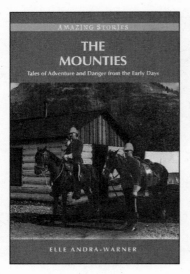

The Mounties
Tales of Adventure and Danger from the Early Days

Elle Andra-Warner

(ISBN 978-1-894974-67-7)

Since 1873, the Mounties have brought the law to the furthest reaches of the Canadian frontier. Sam Steele, the "Lion of the North," was involved in almost every significant event in the Canadian West, while James Macleod and James Walsh negotiated peace with the First Nations peoples. Less famous, unsung heroes risked their lives enforcing justice in the Canadian wilds. From stopping the whisky trade to policing the chaotic gold rush and patrolling the lonely North, these true tales of the early days of the Force are sure to amaze and entertain.

Visit www.heritagehouse.ca to see the entire list of books in this series.

More Great Books in the Amazing Stories Series

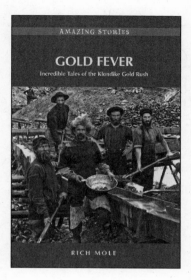

Gold Fever
Incredible Tales of the Klondike Gold Rush

Rich Mole

(ISBN 978-1-894974-69-1)

In 1897, tens of thousands of would-be prospectors flooded into the Yukon in search of instant wealth during the Klondike Gold Rush. In this historical tale of mayhem and obsession, characters like prospectors George Carmack and Skookum Jim, Skagway gangster Soapy Smith and Mountie Sam Steele come to life. Enduring savage weather, unforgiving terrain, violence and starvation, a lucky few made their fortune, and some just as quickly lost it. The lure of the North is still irresistible in this exciting account of a fabled era of Canadian history.

Visit www.heritagehouse.ca to see the entire list of books in this series.

More Great Books in the Amazing Stories Series

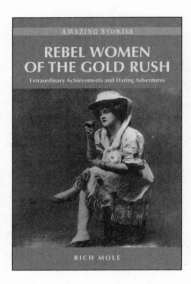

Rebel Women of the Gold Rush
Extraordinary Achievements and Daring Adventures

Rich Mole

(ISBN 978-1-894974-76-9)

Many of the women who arrived in the Klondike longed for the thrill of adventure and an end to the tedium of everyday life, while others sought riches. At a time when women were expected to conform to society's strict rules, the rebel women of the Klondike broke them with gusto, turning dreams into realities. They became millionaires, entrepreneurs, prostitutes, widows, wives, rebels and even murderers, scandalizing society in the process. Often on a trail of heartbreak and false hopes, they came to love the vast, untamed land that played a starring role in their own inspiring stories.

Visit www.heritagehouse.ca to see the entire list of books in this series.

More Great Books in the Amazing Stories Series

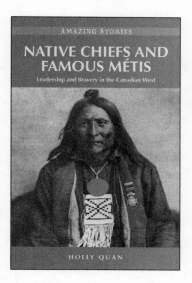

Native Chiefs and Famous Métis
Leadership and Bravery in the Canadian West

Holly Quan

(ISBN 978-1-894974-74-5)

These tales of bravery, courage and decisive action in times of terrible conflict are the stories of heroes. Although the lives of the Native chiefs and famous Métis featured in this book were often tinged with sadness and loss, they were also an inspiration. Full of adventures and battles, these tales ultimately tell of the negotiations, broken promises and harsh realities of the changing face of the West.

Visit www.heritagehouse.ca to see the entire list of books in this series.

More Great Books in the Amazing Stories Series

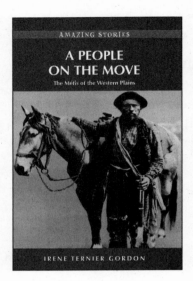

A People on the Move
The Métis of the Western Plains

Irene Ternier Gordon

(ISBN 978-1-894974-85-1)

This book paints a picture of Métis life and culture during the 19th century in the area that later became Saskatchewan and Alberta. Gordon brings history to life through the stories of individuals, such as Gabriel Dumont, and remarkable families, including the Rowand family of Fort Edmonton. The tragedy of 1885, the founding of Willow Bunch and the coming of the NWMP are just some of the key events covered.

Also by Irene Ternier Gordon:

The Battle of Seven Oaks: And the Violent Birth of the Red River Settlement (ISBN 978-1-554390-25-0)

Marie-Anne Lagimodière: The Incredible Story of Louis Riel's Grandmother (ISBN 978-1-551539-67-9)

Visit www.heritagehouse.ca to see the entire list of books in this series.